THE MAGIC OF PSYCHIC POWER

THE MAGIC OF
PSYCHIC POWER

by

DAVID J. SCHWARTZ, Ph.D.

THE AQUARIAN PRESS
Denington Estate, Wellingborough
Northamptonshire

Original American edition published by
Prentice-Hall, Inc., Englewood Cliffs, New Jersey, U.S.A.
Copyright © 1965 by Parker Publishing Company

First U.K. Edition 1967
First U.K. paperback edition 1976
Fourth Impression 1983

ISBN 0 85030 136 X

Printed and bound in Great Britain

CONTENTS

How This Book Can Bring You Wealth And Success Through The Magic Of Psychic Power

This is not an ordinary book. It was not prepared for you to read casually and then pass on to a friend or place on a shelf, never to read again. *The Magic of Psychic Power* is an extraordinary guide to the practical conversion of wisdom into successful living.

Most people—and you are not one of them or you would not be reading this book—most people have utter contempt for that miraculous instrument we call the psyche. The typical person allows this marvelous instrument to go uncared for, undeveloped, uncontrolled.

Such a magnificent thinking apparatus as your brain should guarantee you happiness, prosperity, peace of mind, and success in anything you want to do. It is amazing that there is poverty in a world inhabited by people with psychic power. Harnessing just a fraction of this tremendous influence would erase the problems of man. But poverty is the most tangible example we have that we do not apply wisdom.

I have witnessed many miracles. I have witnessed the joyous

miracle of a young lady confined to a wheel chair attend and succeed in completing college. I have seen the inspiring miracle of an individual with very ordinary background fight insurmountable odds only to win, achieve, and become head of a large corporation. I have seen the thrilling miracle of an individual who had "no chance" rise above and succeed on a grand scale. I have seen miracles in which poor people became rich, sick people became well, little people became big people, defeated people found victory!

But I have also witnessed many miracles of an opposite nature. A miracle is an unusual, unexplainable event. I have seen, for example, the disappointing miracle of a young man born in an upper class family committed to a home for alcoholics before he was thirty. I have seen the tragic miracle of a university graduate, a successful, practicing attorney with a fine family, commit suicide. I have seen the disgusting miracle of a young man with an IQ of 140 drift along in a very mediocre job while all around him our society cries for talented men to move up and beyond. I have seen revolting "miracles" lying in the gutters of our big cities.

In fact, it may be a bigger miracle that people fail than that they succeed. Our world today is built in such a way as to almost guarantee success to those who put forth the right kind of intelligent effort.

1. This book shows you how to obtain riches beyond your most fantastic dreams.

2. This book leads the way to a systematic reorganization of your thinking processes to help you make up for lost time and lost effort.

3. This book shows you hundreds of shortcuts to take to arrive at your destination faster.

4. To you, who seem to have gotten bogged down in a situation in which you are not moving upward, this book will help you discover why and then how to bring about the corrective action.

5. To you, who are troubled with all the many problems of life, this book shows simple but amazingly effective solutions.

6. To you, who want to get more excitement, more positive thrills from life; to you, who want to conquer the boredom and enjoy life, this book shows how.

7. And for those of you who seem to lose more often than you win, this book shows a positive method for winning all the time and never losing.

Hundreds of people who have applied the philosophy explained in detail in this book have learned how to make more money, find more happiness, sell more, rear children more effectively, manage better, influence people, and in many, many other ways get on top of life and make life work for them.

As you read this book, I want you to be alone—physically and spiritually alone. It is a law that genuine wisdom is revealed to us in solitude. Wisdom does not jump out of a TV set into your brain and then into your pattern of behavior. All great thinkers spend considerable periods of time alone, physically and spiritually apart from other people.

Today you often hear people refer to the "Knowledge Explosion." Every ten years it is necessary to double the amount of library space just to house new knowledge. But, unfortunately, while knowledge is expanding at a fantastic rate, practical wisdom—the kind that brings inner satisfaction, love, money, and other good things—is not. Keen, sharp, shrewd wisdom is still in very short supply. Yet, we know this: if we are wise, we are happy. If we are wise, we are successful.

If you are a thinking person, if you are receptive to a formula for converting wisdom into psychic power, this book is for you. If you are tired of being a psychological slave, if you are disgusted with mediocrity, if you are disappointed with your past results, then, my friend, get busy now, right now, for an experience that will alter forever your thought processes.

As a beginning point, remember this: When God made you, he immediately threw away the formula. No one else in this entire world is like you. You are unique. No one else is your equal.

How You Can Have
A Larger Share Of
The Better Things
In Life

1

You are about to start an adventure that will reward you richly for the rest of your life.

You are going to learn new, fresh ways to apply your psychic power to gain more of everything good—more happiness, more love, more money, and more peace of mind.

Nothing in life is more fascinating than understanding—and then harnessing—the amazing power of your psyche. This book shows how. You will enjoy it.

But one favor please. Read this first chapter very slowly. Meditate. Let the concepts sink in. Condition yourself for exposure to genuine wisdom.

Now, if you're ready, let's get going.

As a first step, I want you to visualize a big pie cut in five equal pieces. Next, I want you to visualize five people about to sit down to eat this pie. We'll call the pie "Everything Good in Life"—happiness, love, money, and peace of mind. The five people who are about to eat this pie are five people of similar intelligence, education, and backgrounds.

Now remember, this pie represents "Everything Good in Life." The next thing we must do is divide the pie among the five people. Here we are going to divide the pie in the precise manner that all good things in life are divided. Here's what will happen:

Four of the five people will share one piece of pie. The other person will have four pieces of pie all to himself Imagine! One person of the five will have four times as much pie as the other four people combined.

This is Schwartz's first law. Learn it well: *Eighty percent of everything good is owned by twenty percent or less of the people.* This law, I should add, is conservative. Let's see how it works out. Eighty percent of all of the corporate securities are owned by twenty percent or less of the people. Eighty percent of the real estate is owned by twenty percent or less of the people. Eighty percent of the income is received by twenty percent or less of the people.

Over and over again in many different ways, I have demonstrated this law to be true. I have found, for example, that eighty percent of the scientific breakthrough, the inventions, the significant books, the truly great art of this world are created by twenty percent *or less* of the people. Eighty percent of everything sold is sold by twenty percent or less of the salesmen. Eighty percent of the ideas that have commercial significance are developed by twenty percent or less of the people. Eighty percent of the real fun of life is enjoyed by twenty percent of the people. And there is no doubt about this: Eighty percent of psychological love and physical love is enjoyed by twenty percent or less of the people.

As we examine this law, we see that it applies to everything tangible such as money, stocks, real estate, business and professional success and achievements. But does it also apply to happiness? Again, there is every indication that it does. One family in five enjoys as much happiness as four families combined. All good things are distributed roughly in this 80-20 proportion.

The Schwartz 80-20 Law applies whether we are talking about personal incomes, sales volume, happiness, business success, or any other activity.

It is a law. And you can no more argue with the 80-20 Law than you can argue with the law of gravity. And, like all natural laws, it cannot be repealed. So burn the Schwartz 80-20 Law into your memory.

Now, our next step is to understand "the why" of this law—learn to understand it so you can profit from it instead of being damned by it.

Why does one person in five get four-fifths of the "Everything Good" pie? How does this person differ from the other four? What is the secret? How can you enlarge your share of the pie? How can you become the one in five who enjoys as much as the other four combined? That is what this book shows you how to do.

Experts who study this matter point out that if we divided all the money, all the wealth in our nation among the people equally, it would only be a matter of a few years until the wealth would be owned on the proportionate basis that it is owned now. In other words, if everyone were forced to start over with an equal number of marbles, it would only be a little while until one fellow in five owned four marbles in five.

The fact that income and wealth, even if equally divided, would soon end up very unequally divided proves one thing: that the one person in five who owns eighty percent of all good things is *different* from other people. There is something special about him. What is this something?

Is this enormous difference explained by intelligence—the native ability to think? Success would be simple to explain if it were related directly to intelligence. But it isn't. Nor is success related to health or luck (being at the right place at the right time or knowing the right people).

That intangible something that accounts for the amazing difference in achievement and happiness of people is far more elusive, far more difficult to pin down than something simple like "intelligence quotient," or luck, or education, or childhood advantages.

In a nutshell, the difference is found in the way we plan, organize, and control our psychic power.

Let me repeat. The difference between the successful and the mediocre is found in the way we plan, organize, and control our psychic power.

Let me pause right here to ask you two questions. First, do you understand the 80-20 Law? Second, do you want to join the twenty percent who own the eighty percent? If your answer to each question is "yes," then let's go. If your answer to either question is "no," I'm afraid you are wasting your time and should stop right here.

To Heck With the Mediocre, Middle-Class Philosophy. Don't You Want to Live?

I've asked hundreds of people representing both the successful and the very mediocre to explain their philosophies of life to me. Here is a composite picture of the way that huge, mediocre eighty percent of the people think. Let's call this representative of mediocrity Willie. Here is a condensation of his goals and ambitions:

"I live in an average home. (Every home for as far as my eyes can see looks just about like my home.) I drive an average car —except that I have a few little do-dads which make it just a little different from every other car. Every three or four years I trade that car for another average car.

"Once every summer I will try to take my wife and children on a week's vacation. Then, when we can, we will open up a savings account and save $5 a week and draw four percent interest in a bank. My money will be absolutely safe there and some day I will be what some banks call a 'thousandaire.'

Every other weekend we will invite Bob and Sue to our house. Every other weekend Bob and Sue will invite us to their house.

"I don't like my job, but it pays a living income and makes few demands on me. I won't get rich but I don't want to be rich. [He lies to himself.] The only smart thing to do is go through life taking as few chances as possible. I have no big goals—after all, no one can predict the future.

"The people who have money have had to cheat somebody and I don't want to cheat anyone. I may not have a whole lot, but I am good and they are bad. I won't buy stocks because the stock market could go down and I could lose some money.

"I don't particularly care for my neighbors. But I've got to live beside them, so, I've got to please them. I'm going to try to act like an average person because if I did something unusual, my neighbors would disapprove and I've got to have their approval."

That's the way the Willies in the world think. The Willies go to bed at about the same time every night, get up the same time every morning, eat exactly the same breakfast, grunt the same grunts, gripe the same gripes, drive to work over the same streets, greet their co-workers the same pessimistic way, eat lunch in the same dirty, depressing place, do the same work, go home the same way, eat about the same dinner. Then, after the dull, depressing day, they gather up all their energy and move into the den to watch the same TV program they watched one week before.

Those are the Willies. And remember, eighty percent of the people you know belong in the Willie classification.

The Philosophy of the Elite

Now, let's take a look at the philosophy that is followed by the small elite twenty percent that move ahead and enjoy life. Let's call this composite individual Charlie.

First of all, Charlie realizes life is too short to be little. He doesn't go out of his way to offend his neighbors, but at the same time he really doesn't care what they think. He's much more concerned about what *he* thinks and about what *he* wants.

If his neighbor mows his lawn twice a week, this doesn't bother brother Charlie. Charlie mows his yard as often as he wants to mow his yard.

Charlie feels equal to other people. He has a job that pays him in proportion to what he produces. If he produces more through ambition and talent, he expects to be paid more. Deep down, he feels he is captain of his own fate.

Charlie takes vacations not just once a year but as often as possible. Charlie and his family rarely do exactly the same thing twice. He is curious. He wants to experiment. He likes, in a psychological sense, living dangerously. He does different and exciting things.

Very importantly, Charlie is not worried about "security," "the future," "tomorrow." Charlie is confident he can handle any situation that comes up. He realizes that security comes from within, not from without.

At work, Charlie defends his title every day. He's not afraid of people who may be pushing him—fact is, he enjoys competition since it makes his job interesting. Charlie is a pro. He likes competing with his own potential instead of trying to beat second-classers.

Charlie drives the kind of car he wants to drive, goes where he wants to go, enjoys his family, and lives to get kicks out of life. He learned the wisdom of the great philosopher, Disraeli—"Life is too short to be little."

Charlie avoids the dull routine. He does things to break up the monotony of life and keep himself fresh.

Charlie looks forward to the future, not as some point in the distance when he can sit on the sand in Old Folksville, Florida, and do nothing, but rather as a point in time when he will have achieved his predetermined goals. Charlie takes chances because he realizes a law of nature is uncertainty. Charlie follows a map in life.

Charlie is not concerned about how much money his neighbors make—*Charlie is concerned about how much money HE makes.* Charlie is not interested in living in peace to the extent that he does not have these problems.

Charlie avoids the hallway, the restaurant, and the rest room conversations about the boss and his mixed up marital relations. Charlie is interested exclusively in *his* marital relationship—in *his* sex life.

There you have two diametrically opposed philosophies. And it is this difference in philosophy which explains why life pays Charlie four times as much as life pays Willie. Willie is a slave, a conformist, a modern-day, middle-class peasant, a psychological slave. Charlie is a free man, a doer, and a modern-day king.

Here's a test you can apply. Select five people you know well. Then see if four of these five do not belong in the Willie classification.

Eighty percent have surrendered their psychic power to the masses. Eighty percent have decided not to live but to let other people control their thinking. Eighty percent have surrendered.

When things go wrong, the Willies blame their wife (or their boss, some politician, their employees). The Willies always easily find a scapegoat to blame for their own problems. It never dawns on the Willies that they may have some inadequacy which causes the problem.

Meanwhile, the Charlies are not blaming the wife, or the boss, or the employees, or the federal government in Washington. Charlie has reached true psychological maturity—he holds himself accountable for his own mistakes. And in doing this, Charlie establishes himself as a man who can grow and rise to higher and higher levels of responsibility.

Case Histories of Four Bad and One Good Miracle

Some years ago I attended the fifteenth anniversary of my university class. Fifteen years is long enough to see definite trends take place in the lives of people.

Over a Friday through Sunday weekend, I had an opportunity to visit individually and at considerable length with five friends whom I had known very well at college. Each of these individuals started out with great ambitions, great dreams, and great hopes.

These were individuals who shared the same experiences, knew the same people. In those long-ago days we had talked about the things most college people talk about—success, love, jobs, world peace, the future, God, politics. But most of all, we talked about where we were going and how we were going to get there. We did our share of philosophizing about life. And we had dreams of what we used to refer to as the "really good, good life."

Let me give you a quick capsule report about what happened to each of these five people. Perhaps they will remind you of some of your old friends.

Let's take a look.

Case #1. Hardened, angry, bitter Mrs. F. M. Mrs. F. M., 36, is married to a physician, has two children, and is extremely unhappy. Mrs. F. M. was exceptionally well-dressed and appeared very poised. But her eyes are mean and cruel. And her face shows she has forgotten how to laugh and enjoy life.

"About all my education did was make me unhappy," she commented. "I'd have been way ahead if I'd never learned about what's going on in the world," she added bitterly.

"I live in a town I can't stand. I don't like the people. There's no place to go except to stupid things like P.T.A. and the bridge club. I have no fun. Being a doctor's wife I've got to be on guard all the time.

"Oh, I suppose my husband is happy," Mrs. F. M. explained.

"After all he's got his practice and he buries himself in it. But I'm not. I don't think I love him any more, but I've got two children and I live for them.

"Oh, I guess I put on a pretty good front. I suppose the people who know me think we're a happy couple. That's one thing I've got to give my education credit for—it taught me how to look one way but feel another.

"You know," she added, "I feel like I've been sentenced to a psychological prison, and it looks like I'm there for life."

Now note. This is the same woman who, only fifteen years before, had big goals for being a first-rate anthropologist. She wanted to make the world a better place. In school, she had often talked about working for the United Nations or the State Department.

But now she was totally frustrated. Most of her warm attractiveness, which was once so exceptional, was gone. Money was not her problem. Being married to a respected physician eliminated status in her community as a problem. Mrs. F. M.'s trouble was that she felt enslaved. She was a "slave" to a career she didn't like, to a husband she didn't love, and to a future that was totally pessimistic. Her only source of joy was two children. But is this enough?

Mrs. F. M.'s martini glass never stayed full long. Unless there is major psychic surgery soon, she'll have other major problems to compound those she already faces.

Case #2. Phoney, fakey Pete. Pete, back in college, had been one of those interesting characters that succeeds in amusing just about everyone. The old gang used to think he was exceedingly clever, sharp, and a real smart character. Pete, even then, demonstrated his philosophy toward life. Pete believed the outside world was stupid. All you needed to do, he thought, was adopt a phoney, con-man approach and swindle yourself to success.

Pete had not lost his ability to talk. He spent his weekend telling everyone about the big deals he had pulled off in stocks and real estate, the big gambles he had taken and won, the big accomplishments he had made. But Pete talked so much and in such a way that the inconsistencies in what he said were obvious. Pete hadn't succeeded in anything.

The truth about Pete's "success" pieced together from other sources boiled down to this: He was all talk and nothing more. His net worth was nil and his bank credit had long ago been shut off. Pete had been in and out of many things but had never been psychologically committed to anything.

Pete is one of those someday-my-ship-will-come-in people. His wife, Jean, devotes herself to trying to keep Pete going, and a second look at her shows the enormous strain she is under.

Everything about Pete showed that his confidence—which had always been artificial—was gone. Pete had no purpose. Pete was committed to nothing. Today, Pete is, in plain talk, an educated bum.

The problem here is that Pete still hasn't learned the truth. Pete still feels the phoney front is the secret to success. Pete doesn't lack basic intelligence. And he has enough ambition, though it is misdirected. Pete is afraid of himself and has become a psychological slave devoted to uncoordinated, undirected daydreaming.

Case #3. Bill T.—Man who surrendered completely. Fifteen years before Bill T. had been one of the most promising individuals in his class—intelligent, conscientious, and eager to succeed.

But fifteen years later, Bill T. has convinced himself that life is like a jail sentence—something to be served. Bill is psychologically dead. His drive, his striving for fun and achievement is gone. Bill is a psychic robot performing work far below his ability. Bill has developed a warped, twisted view of life.

"We got a bum steer here at the University," he told me. "People shouldn't be taught to want or expect happiness. They ought to teach these kids (here he waved in the general direction of the dormitories on the main campus) that this is a tough world and they shouldn't expect to like it.

"Let's be honest," Bill emphasized, "life is a struggle—something to *endure*, not enjoy."

Here Bill went on a real negative kick (and I might add the only thing Bill could get enthusiastic about was the awful, negative side of life.) Bill took apart the modern corporation and how unfair it was, the cheats he had met in business, the dishonesty in politics, the trend toward leftism, and all the other revolting things in our society.

Then Bill explained his solution to me. "I finally had enough sense to give up. I discovered how stupid the old idea, that if you work hard, you'll get ahead really is. So six years ago I got myself a job with Civil Service and stopped fighting the system."

"How do you like it?" I asked.

"I don't," he replied. "But it pays me enough to live in a respectable middle class suburb. And I've learned to try to find satisfactions in other things. But the important thing is, I don't expect happiness so I'm not going to be disappointed.'

In a word, Bill T. surrendered. He is trying to go through life on a pass and is avoiding all the real stuff life is made of. He is a "drop out" from the College of Life.

Part of Bill's problem is that he never learned that problems are the source of life's excitement. Bill still doesn't realize that the only people who have no problems have already been admitted to a cemetery.

Case #4. Wrong Career Tim—But "It's Too Late Now." Another old friend I met at the college round up I'll refer to here as Tim. Tim had gone through the College of Engineering. I remembered him as an exceptionally conscientious, sincere fellow who had studied hard, done well, and maintained a good record.

But Tim had lost all that old drive—all that dedication to winning.

After we were relaxed Tim said to me, "You know, Dave, I made only one big mistake since college and believe me, it's a big one."

"What was it?" I asked, half-thinking he'd tell me about a bad investment or a disappointing marriage.

"Well," he said, "I never really liked engineering. Remember how hard I used to study? I did finish o.k. and by all that damn work came out in the top third of the class.

"I took a job with the X Engineering Company and I've been there ever since. I soon acquired family responsibilities and felt I couldn't afford to get into something else. Over the years every job I was offered paid less to start than I was making. So I stayed with it.

"Now," Tim went on, "life is just a hum-drum experience. I know now I should have gotten into sales or management. But it's too late to make the change."

"Why?" I asked, thinking that it's never too late to start something else.

"Well, Dave, to be perfectly honest," he went on, "I'm scared to make a change. I'd have to compete with guys who are younger and a lot fresher than I. So, I'm stuck."

That was Tim. Still under 40, yet afraid to correct a mistake made 15 years before. And, as is true in all such cases, the longer he waits, the more he will be a slave to his own self-developed fear.

Tim, I know, had heard hundreds of brilliant lectures. But he missed the one which points out that the only way to conquer fear is to do the thing one fears. Unless Tim grabs hold and makes a change now by the time the thirtieth anniversary rolls around, Tim will be a truly pathetic case.

Case #5. Mighty Mike—The Sleeper Who Came Through. Mike was the one in the old crowd who pulled the big upset. In college, Mike always was a "good guy" but didn't excel in social life or in the academic. Mike didn't have much money and he worked at various odd jobs much of the time. Mike was more of a doer than a talker.

Since college, Mike, I learned, had had his share of "downs" but he chose not to view them as such. He had run for Congress once and gotten smashed. He had developed one business only to see it go under. Mike had experienced several personal tragedies including the death of a young child.

But now, through a positive, keep-trying spirit, Mike had built up a very successful brokerage firm, dealing in securities, owned a major size ranch in Colorado, two car dealerships, and a variety of other interests. Mike had a happy wife, four kids, had been to Europe several times, and had flown his own plane to the alumni reunion. He was living life and enjoying every minute of it.

In one of those corner-of-the-room discussions, I asked Mike to tell me how he managed to achieve so much despite the early problems. Mike said, "Well, after I finished school I gradually developed a cornerstone for a personal philosophy.

"What is it?" I asked.

"Just this. I've trained myself to believe, absolutely, completely believe, that all things work together for good. For example, when I ran for Congress and got beaten, I saw the good side. I learned a hell of a lot in that campaign. In a way, I was the winner even though I lost the election.

"And when my first business venture failed, I just chalked it up to education. If I hadn't failed so miserably the first time, I wouldn't have been so successful in later ventures."

I'm sure the college test scores would show that Mike was not as smart as some of the others. But he had learned what it takes to find happiness and satisfaction in the world around him. Mike had learned how to win and win even when he appeared to lose.

Why Are Four Out of Five Psychological Slaves?

That Sunday evening as I boarded my jet I had mixed feelings. I had had a close-up look at the end of 15 laps of five people closely matched in terms of intelligence, preparation, and opportunity, who entered life's race together.

Each of these people had excellent academic preparation. Each had plenty of intelligence. Each had lived in a long, continuous economic boom. But only one of the five had honestly conquered life. I had seen another living example of the 80-20 Law in action.

But why? What had gone wrong? Four of my five old friends had committed what I call the seven deadly psychic sins. Read these sins below and read them carefully. Remember, the wages of psychic sin is psychological death.

Seven Deadly Psychic Sins That Produce Failures

An analysis of failures—the eighty percent who are caught in the grip of psychological slavery, mediocre achievement, boredom, and frustration—an analysis of these people shows they commit day in and day out seven deadly psychological sins.

Here they are. Check each one carefully. These are the sins that explain why four out of five people spin their mental gears and end up in the land of nowhere.

Sin #1. Letting other people run your life instead of managing it yourself so you can do what you want to do. Committing this sin means you surrender to the dictates of second-class people. You let them pull you down to their level of mediocre income, mediocre achievement, and mediocre happiness.

Second-class people say, "You ought to do this," so you do it. Second-class people dictate the kind of job you should have, the way you should perform on that job, the way you should behave in your private life. Misguided husbands, domineering wives, over-bearing employers, and interfering relatives frequently are these "other people" who run your life.

One way to find out whether you are committing this sin is to analyze the most recent decision you made. Did you choose what you wanted to choose? Or did you choose it on the basis of what other people might think?

Sin #2. Blaming other people for your bad "luck" and tough "breaks" instead of blaming yourself. The individual with the disciplined psyche creates the circumstances that influence him.

But most people do not have a disciplined psyche. Napoleon once said, "Circumstances? I create the circumstances that affect me." So it is with successful people. This sin of finding a scapegoat is so easy it's deceptive. People you know commit this sin when they analyze why they aren't getting ahead at work, or why they are not selling, or why they make low grades, or why someone else moves up the ladder while they stay near the bottom. Sin #2 is a bad one. You'll discover, as you study this textbook of psychic management, the rewards that come to individuals who succeed in avoiding this psychic sin.

Sin #3. Selling your ability short—showing subconscious contempt for your own potential. Without exception, the failures in this world think they are inadequate, think they will finish last in the race, and think the good, wonderful things in life are beyond their grasp.

It's often said, "Familiarity breeds contempt." So it is with the respect we show for our own brain power. Every day tens of thousands of people think original, creative, worthwhile ideas only to dismiss the idea because it came from their brain. It's so easy to commit this sin. In truth, we make two big mistakes about intelligence. We grossly exaggerate other people's intelligence and we grossly underestimate our own.

Sin #4. Allowing fear to dominate every phase of your life. Fear of other people, fear of giving something a try, fear of economic disaster, fear of self—these are some of the common fears of people who commit this psychologically deadly sin.

Fear, not confidence, rules the world. Fear is behind all failure.

Sin #5. Failing to manage and direct your psychic processes— to organize your mind to achieve goals. That great horde of sec-

2

ond and third-class performers have this in common—they have no real purpose for being alive. They mentally drift, they do wishful thinking instead of purposeful thinking.

Only a very, very few people have bothered to write down on paper what they expect to accomplish. Only a very few have a will for living. They drift, disorganized, not knowing where they are or worse still, where they are going. They are taking a trip through life with no map. As a result, that powerful device—the brain—fails to perform at anything near maximum output.

Sin #6. Becoming so involved in yourself and your fictional inadequacies that you cannot learn the magic secrets for winning command of others. Success requires the ability to influence other people. But this ability can't be developed if you are completely involved in thinking only about yourself.

In today's complex society, you must be able to persuade other people to your point of view if you want to achieve at a high level. But nearly everyone commits this sin. Nearly everyone asks himself, "What's in it for me?" instead of asking, "What can I do for the other person?" Successful folks know if you want to get you've got to give.

Sin #7. Failing to believe—fully, completely believe—that you can make your mind function the way you want it to function. Failing to believe that you *can* win, that you *can* succeed, that you *can* earn more money, have more influence, achieve real peace of mind is this sin in action.

Nearly everyone has heard some version of the philosophy, "Faith will move mountains," hundreds of times. But here again, the typical person you know shows contempt for this great wisdom. He knows that faith doesn't work. The person who achieves controls his thinking. He doesn't let his thinking control him.

The Time to Start is NOW.

I hope at this point you are ready to say, "I want to move up, out, and beyond. I want to find more happiness. I want to enjoy the good life. I want to succeed." If you are ready to make that commitment, then let me urge you to start now.

Here's a game I often play when I'm presenting a clinic to a small group. I pick out one individual who looks like a good sport and say to him: "Sir, I'm going to ask you a question and I must have your answer in three seconds, okay?" (I impose the three second rule because I am after a top-of-the-head opinion, which is usually the only level on which people think.)

"Sir," I continue, "a baby was born just a few minutes ago in a nearby hospital. Now, before I count to three, tell me what you feel is the approximate life expectancy of that baby in days."

The most frequent response I get is, "I've never thought of it that way, but I'd guess, oh, about 100,000 days."

I use this illustration to demonstrate how little respect most people have for life itself. The correct answer is approximately 25,500 days. Yet, most people—even engineers with years and years of slide rule experience—will typically guess 100,000 days. (Now, anyone born a 100,000 days ago would have been born about eighty years before George Washington was elected President!)

Talk about a strict rationing board! Life is about the tightest "commodity" available. Only 25,500 days on the average.

When you think of it this way you begin to appreciate what Disraeli meant when he said, "Life is too short to be little."

Today—and every day—roughly 5500 Americans die. In a year, our total death toll is equal to twice the population of metropolitan Atlanta. Now, death itself isn't sad because it is a natural thing that must happen to each of us. Death is just as much a part of nature's plan as is birth. What is sad is the fact that most of these 5500 people who will die today never really enjoyed the trip!

Most of these people spent their precious moments fighting to survive instead of living on a big scale; most behaved like cowards afraid to speak up, afraid of criticism; most of them had dreams once but watched these dreams shrivel up and die.

Many if not most of these people were never psychologically born.

AS A STARTER, COMMIT THESE CONCEPTS TO MEMORY

1. Eighty percent of everything good—happiness, love, money, peace of mind—is owned by twenty percent or less of the people.

2. The one person in five who has four marbles in five has no better advantages in terms of intelligence, education, luck, or opportunity. He leads the pack because he controls his psychic power.

3. The multitude of mediocre people commit seven deadly psychic sins. They are

    (a)   let other people run their lives
    (b)   blame luck for their bad breaks
    (c)   underestimate their potential
    (d)   surrender to fear instead of conquering it
    (e)   fail to set clear goals
    (f)   fail to learn how to persuade other people
    (g)   think defeat instead of think victory

4. Life is tightly rationed. Better start living right now!

How To Break
The Bonds
Of Psychological
Slavery

2

Only a little over a hundred years ago there was still a great deal of slavery in the United States. Some human beings were actually owned by other human beings. They were bought and sold and treated in much the same manner as cattle.

Physical slavery—that type of slavery by which you could be owned and completely controlled *physically* by other human beings—is dead.

But insofar as you are concerned, an even worse form of slavery exists today. I call it psychological slavery. It's a form of bondage in which the vast majority of people owe their souls to someone else. It's a form of slavery which finds people doing work they hate, living in an environment which they don't like, going places they don't want to go, doing things against their will, and in many, many other ways surrendering to the will of other people.

People who enjoy the good life, people who climb ahead,

people who get where they like to go, are psychologically free. This chapter shows you how you can escape from psychological prisons which have been built around you. Let's look now at how you can conquer six specific forms of psychological slavery:

1. "What will other people think of me?" slavery.
2. "I'm certain to fail" slavery.
3. "It's too late" slavery.
4. "I'm a slave to security" slavery.
5. "Past mistakes" slavery.
6. "I'm trapped by my environment" slavery.

"What will other people think of me?" slavery

Perhaps the five words in the English language which do most to enslave people are these: "What will other people think?"

"What will other people think?" is one of the most common —and destructive—forms of psychological slavery. It ranges all the way from "I've got to mow my lawn once a week because if I don't the neighbors will think I'm shiftless"; to "I won't say anything at the meeting because the others will think I'm just trying to make points"; to "We've got to go to the party or it won't look right"; to "I can't wear that. If I do, they'll laugh at me."

"Other people" slavery is strong, powerful. "Other people" slavery explains why there is so much conformity in the world. It helps explain why too many women fix their hair like other women; why most salesmen sell just alike (and are, therefore, strictly ordinary in the money earned column); why people live boring, unhappy, unsatisfying lives.

"Other people" slavery kills your creativity and your personality. It destroys your ability to have the kind of fun *you* like, to go where *you* want to go, to do the things you want to do.

Not only are most people slaves to "what other people think," but they also make the stupid error of listening to the advice of other unqualified people.

Advice is everywhere and most of it is free. Your neighbor,

your relatives, your associates, just about everyone you know is eager to advise you. You have perhaps a dozen or more unpaid voluntary "consultants" on your self-management staff. These consultants, even without your asking for it, advise you on everything from rearing children to caring for your health to making your investments.

Psychologically immature people follow the advice of these self-appointed consultants, who usually know little of what they talk about. Rather than trust their own judgment or seek the advice of a competent, trained person, these people listen to and follow suggestions of second-class people.

Is it any wonder the advice is usually wrong?

Accepting advice from just anybody who happens to be around is like taking a fine new Sting Ray to an alley garage to be worked on. You are too important to be worked on by an alley-type advisor. Go first class in selecting your consultants to serve on your self-management task.

Now, even when you visit paid consultants like lawyers and accountants, use your own judgment as a final check.

I've made this a steadfast rule. I seek the comments and suggestions of big people—people who know from experience. The other critics I dismiss completely. They aren't important to me.

At first I paid a great deal of attention to what someone else might say. I wanted to please everyone. Then I learned a magnificent lesson. *Measure the size of your critic before you pay much attention to what the critic has to say.*

A management expert recently gave me his views on what it takes to be a leader.

"Everybody keeps telling us we should try to be normal. But the normal guy goes nowhere, does nothing. Leadership, by definition, means someone who is different from the group. You can't be "normal" and be a leader. Certain qualities must stand out. It's plain stupid to think of normalcy and leadership as being the same. In a way, what we should be doing is trying to differentiate ourselves from other people instead of making ourselves exactly like other people.

Here's a four-way approach to attaining freedom from "other people" slavery:

1. "Other people" aren't pacemakers—they're followers. If you feel you'd be delightfully happy if you could copy your neighbors one hundred percent, then copy them. Otherwise, live your life and let them live theirs. As long as what you do does no physical or spiritual harm to others, do as you please.

2. You're really not anybody until somebody hates you. The bigger you grow, the more critics you'll have, the more you'll be gossiped about. Criticism by "other people" is a sign you are envied.

3. Choose friends who aren't "other people" conscious. This helps break your fear of what other people think. Associate with "live and let live" people.

4. Remember, these "other people" usually have more problems of their own than they can cope with. (The married couple who is afraid "other people" will learn about their quarrels would be amazed if they could see the quarreling that the "other people" are doing.)

"I'm certain to fail" slavery

Here is another exceedingly common form of psychological slavery. People who have surrendered to this kind of slavery continually think "I haven't got a chance," "I'll fail," "I can't get the better job," "I can't earn more money," "The whole world is against me," "My boss doesn't think much of me," and on, and on, and on.

All of the defeated slaves in this category have this in common. They have an unfavorable self-concept. They think little of themselves. They cannot see themselves in true perspective.

Internationally respected Dr. Walter C. Reckless, an Ohio State sociologist, decided several years ago to try and find out why the lives of two boys from the same slum often turn out so radically different. One may become a great surgeon or a successful business man. The other may become a hunted criminal.

To do this research, Dr. Reckless selected two groups of sixth grade boys in two elementary schools in Columbus, Ohio that were known as delinquency areas.

One group was considered "trouble prone" by teachers, parents, and friends. The other group was selected as "non-trouble prone."

Over a period of five years the two groups panned out as anticipated. The "good" boys kept out of trouble and the potentially "bad" boys got into trouble (over 39 percent had been in juvenile court an average of three times).

Now, here's the most significant feature of this research: The "bad" group of boys *expected in advance of any difficulty* to get into trouble. The typical boy in this category *believed* he would get in trouble with the law; he felt his friends would get in trouble; he doubted that he would finish school; he believed his family was no good, and so on.

Meanwhile, the "good" category of boys had just the opposite viewpoint. The youngster in this group *believed* he would stay out of trouble; he *believed* he would succeed in school; he *believed* his family was for him, and so on.

In the words of Dr. Reckless, "We concluded that slum boys at threshold age (12) who had an *unfavorable self-concept* were most vulnerable to delinquency."

Now, there you have a carefully conducted research study that proves "thinking *does* make it so." You can apply this discovery in other directions too. For example—

The girl who *thinks* she is ugly gets uglier; the girl who *thinks* she is beautiful gets more beautiful.

The young lawyer going into practice for himself who thinks he'll fail at best will be only mediocre. Meanwhile, his companion who feels he will succeed in private practice almost invariably does.

Only a miracle can produce a victory for the football team that "knows it will get beat."

The excessive smoker who gives up cigarettes telling himself, "I know I can't quit," never does.

"I'm certain to lose" slaves can cure themselves, but it takes a change of thinking.

The law is clear: "As a man thinketh, so is he."

Here's how to break the bonds of "I'm certain to fail" slavery:

1. *Hold positive chats with yourself.* During an average day you spend perhaps 100 minutes talking with someone else. If you speak at about the average speed, you say between 10,000 and 20,000 words in a typical day.

That sounds like a lot, doesn't it? But here is a surprising thing. These ten to twenty thousand words are only a small fraction of the words you "speak" to yourself.

Talk is merely verbalized thinking. Sentences are just thoughts expressed in language. But most of your thoughts—the products of your brain factory—are never spoken to someone else. *You speak them only to yourself.* Most of your thinking is directed solely at yourself. It's what "I" says to "Me" that counts. It's not what the fellow at the next desk, or the customer, or the boss says to you that counts most. The really important thing is what your "I" says to your "Me."

Now, here is the point. When you talk to yourself, use good positive language. Think why you can, not why you can't.

Notice the key words Emerson used in commenting on the problems of individuals: "He (man) dismisses his own ideas without notice because the ideas are his." This is another way of saying that familiarity with your own mind breeds contempt for your own ideas.

2. *Think "I'm going to succeed—not fail."* When you think you'll succeed, your mind amazingly begins to find the solution for success.

3. *Think "I'm a winner" not "I'm a loser."* Adopt a little of the Cassius Clay philosophy in this connection. Cassius, over a long period of time, told himself he was the greatest until at least he had convinced himself, and that in the final analysis is the only

person you'll have to convince. Other people are automatically convinced you're great after you have convinced yourself.

"It's too late" slavery

This slavery goes something like this: "I've already had my chance, but I missed it. So, I am stuck and I'll just have to try and make the best of a bad situation."

A 40-year-old bachelor I know told me about his problem. "I'd like very much to get married," he said, "but I realize I'm too old for that sort of thing." (His prospective bride was 27.)

I asked him why. His explanation fit the usual pattern—fear of "not being able to 'adapt,'" fear of "premature death," fear of "insufficient potency," fear of "looking ridiculous to her friends," fear of "being regarded as a grandpa instead of a father to any children who might result."

This fellow summed it up this way, "I just think I'm too old."

To this I had no choice but to tell him, "Well, if you think you're too old, you are." (Careful probing on my part revealed that this fellow had been a slave to the "I'm too old" disease since his mid-twenties. It was only after considerable directed effort that this fellow was able to break free of his psychological enslavement.)

The "It's too late" form of psychological slavery crops up in many other situations. Just last month I had a long discussion with a utility engineer.

"I had my big chance about 12 years ago," he said. "I answered an ad in the *Wall Street Journal* offering a partnership in a new electronics company some guy was setting up outside of Boston. I had enough money and the idea really appealed to me. But I just didn't go ahead with it."

"Why?" I asked.

"Well," he replied, "I had a job paying pretty well at the time. And I just didn't think I ought to give up one bird in the hand for two in the bush. As it turned out, I'd be a millionaire if I'd have gone ahead.

"But now," he continued, "I realize it's too late. A chance like that will never come my way again. And besides, I've got too much time with my company now. I can retire in 14 more years."

This fellow convinced himself he was too old to get started. He has surrendered to 14 more years of slavery and now he's trying to make the best of it.

"It's too late" slaves include a surprising number of people such as the 26-year-old who thinks he's too old to start college, the 42-year-old widow who thinks she's too old to remarry, the 50-year-old professor who thinks he's too old to sacrifice his tenure at a school he hates and join a faculty where he'd be happy, the individual who regrets not having bought common stocks 10 years ago but is convinced that it's too late to invest now.

Slaves to "It's too late now" are victims of old-fashioned thinking—the thinking that said, "There is an age when one should do this and another age when one should do that."

Here's how to break age slavery:

1. Age slavery can be broken just by looking around at that small but alive group who simply ignore it!
2. Decide to live until you die.

"I'm a Slave to Security"

The extent of this kind of slavery is enormous. Many people even fight to achieve security. Yet, the more security we have the less psychological freedom we can enjoy.

The dramatic success of Steve McQueen, the famous star of TV and movies, illustrates how to overcome psychological slavery. Steve had one of those "problem childhoods." He never knew his father. At 14 Mr. McQueen was such a problem child he was placed in a correctional institution.

After a hitch in the Marines he went to New York and did all sorts of odd jobs. One day a friend urged him to try acting. In relatively short order he was a success.

When asked why Steve McQueen became such a success, his

discoverer, Sanford Meisner, said, ". . . I think it was his original personality. He insisted on being himself."

Steve himself outlines three rules he follows in his success achievement program.

> "Rule one: Be yourself—dare to be an individual. Don't try to copy someone else's style.
> "Rule two: Study and work to improve yourself in your profession.
> "Rule three: Have a positive mental attitude and the courage to try. In other words, dare to take a chance." [1]

Note the words, "dare to take a chance."

If all you want is complete security, here is some advice for you. Go live in some public institution—an insane asylum, a poor house, a jail. There you can be certain of a roof over your head, three meals a day, clothes to wear, and cigarette money. You will have absolutely no concerns regarding keeping body and soul together.

Psychological slaves to security have this in common. They lack a controlled imagination. They turn on their imaginations to the mental TV station that has bad news about themselves. They build up monsters and this is not difficult to do. If you wanted to, in less than one hour's time you could conceive of literally thousands of bad things which can happen to you. Meanwhile, at the opposite side, the people who are aiming to get someplace have controlled imaginations. They visualize good things happening to them. They visualize themselves having happiness, having money, having respect, having all the things that truly count.

Ever notice what stimulates children? Children are more stimulated by surprises than by anything else. Kids love to be surprised. But what we do as we fight for security is to destroy surprises. We eliminate the risks and we therefore eliminate the surprises. Is it any wonder that life gets to be so boring for so many of us? The human being is built to struggle.

---

[1] As reported in *Success Unlimited*, February 1964, pp. 6 and 7.

Now, here's the solution to overcoming the "slave to security" problem: *Learn to like living dangerously.*

A lot of people love physical thrills. Go to any state fair and watch them lined up, paying their money to be scared half to death on some kind of roller coaster or other ride. Now, what we need is to apply this to psychic thrills. A good salesman learns to like matching wits.

A good engineer likes a problem that has no easy solution; a top politician goes for broke every day; a success-oriented young couple doesn't fear next month's bills; a good student likes the unannounced pop quizz.

A good speaker loves to run into an audience every once in awhile that is negative, that has to be wrestled with to get livened up. In my own speaking experience, I naturally like to have an audience that's already warmed up. But I find my greatest thrill and accomplishment comes from talking to a large group of people who have had a two-hour "social hour" (that's a modern-day game in which people see who can get drunk first). Anybody, I figure, can speak to the two-drink audience, but friend, when you can talk to an audience that has had four or five martinis before you start speaking, then you know you've got a challenge!

Learn to like the difficult. Learn to like the unusual. Learn to like the unknown.

"I'm a Slave to Past Mistakes"

A lot of psychological slaves are afraid to try again because some place along the line they lost. What every individual interested in controlling his psyche must learn is to develop a philosophy toward making mistakes.

A friend explained it to me this way: "You know, every so often when I'm in Florida I go to the horse races. I put $10 down on Sally, a 40-to-1 shot. Well, if Sally wins I win—I get $400. But if Sally loses, I still win. I get $400 worth of education in why not to gamble for a bargain price of only $10."

Isn't this a terrific philosophy? We all know that education is a requirement these days for success. If we regard our losses as valuable education, they aren't losses at all. They're investments.

Not long ago I talked to a man who had been in business for himself, then failed. He told me he didn't fail at all—he simply learned he didn't want to spend his life in business for himself. Now he's happy doing something else. Most people who fail in business view it just the opposite—as proof they should crawl into a psychological hole and never try again.

It's said Thomas Edison conducted 10,000 experiments to make the first light bulb. But, according to Edison, "These weren't failures. I simply discovered 9,999 ways it wouldn't work."

Don't regard "mistakes" as mistakes. If you are intelligent enough to realize a mistake, it isn't a mistake at all—it's education. So, since you love education, you're actually *glad* you made the mistake.

Blessed is he who is not discouraged by mistakes. Blessed is he who is glad he makes mistakes.

Winning—or losing—is a state of mind.

A prize fighter with only one professional fight to his credit told me what he felt was the greatest prize fight victory of all time. "What was that?" I asked, half-way expecting to hear him tell about the Tunney-Dempsey fight or a Joe Louis battle or maybe a Liston fight.

"In my opinion," he said, "the greatest fight of all time was the fight in which I got knocked cold in the first round. It was the greatest fight of all time because I learned in one night that I shouldn't be a pro boxer.

"Just think," he continued, "if I hadn't gotten smashed that night, I might have drifted along and tried to be a boxer. I'd have been a second-rate boxer."

Don't you begin to believe that all things do work together for good? Think about this the next time you lose out.

If you lose your job, it's good. You shouldn't be in a situation where you aren't suited. Flunk a course in school? Deserted by a lover? Lose money in a stock market? Have a flooded basement?

Come out second in a race? Lose an election?—all of these "misfortunes" are misfortunes only when we think they are misfortunes.

Losing is good if you interpret the loss properly.

William Bolitho, writer for the *Manchester Guardian* early this century, said, "The most important thing in life is not to capitalize on your gains. Any fool can do that. The really important thing is to profit from your losses."

Let me tell you about the most valuable lesson I learned about investing in common stocks. A number of years ago, a real for sure con artist came to me with a tremendous lead about a stock that was certain to quadruple in price in just a few weeks. The price was $4.75 a share.

So, making the stupid mistake of having more confidence in his judgment than in my own, I said, "Buy me a hundred shares." He did and from that day on the stock dropped. Finally, two years after I had purchased the stock I decided I might as well sell it, take my loss, and learn my lesson. I sold stock which had cost me $475 for a grand total of $16. Now, this was a heck of a big lesson. It taught me this: (1) ignore the guy who wants to give me a hot tip, (2) check into a company carefully before I buy it, (3) sell it if it starts dropping too much.

Now many people have had similar experiences. But one such experience drives a lot of people out of the investment market permanently. But, fortunately, instead of regarding the loss as a loss, I regarded it as a very wonderful part of my education. It taught me a great deal and I'm very glad it happened.

"I'm Trapped by my Environment" Slavery

Your environment includes all of those things that surround you. Your environment, probably more than you can realize, shapes your attitudes, viewpoints, and philosophy toward life.

For many people, environment is a form of psychological

imprisonment—something that shades initiative, kills desire, warps the personality.

The case of Mrs. J. B. illustrates this form of psychological slavery. Mrs. J. B., an exceptionally attractive, intelligent, and ambitious woman of 26 presented this problem to me not long ago.

"Dr. Schwartz," she stated very quickly, "I'm married, have three wonderful children—the oldest is five and the baby is two— and I don't love my husband. He says he loves me but I don't think he does. I think he's just a coward afraid to shift for himself."

She paused and was about to cry so I said to her, "Go on, tell me all about it."

"I've got a good job and I love it," she continued, "but divorce is out of the question. And [here she half-smiled] I can't murder him—there's the law. Oh, I've thought of committing suicide, but I can't, not with the children. And besides, I'm young and I would like to live, really live."

As Mrs. J. B.'s story unfolded it became clear to me that this was one of those truly sad cases of a marriage that was bad for all concerned—the children, the wife, the husband, the respective families, their friends, and their co-workers.

I continued probing the problem in depth. I listened to a mountain of evidence all of which added up to total incompatibility.

Finally, I asked Mrs. J. B., "You mentioned a few minutes ago that divorce was out of the question. Why?"

This took some digging. While her religion permitted divorce under her circumstances and appeared justified in her case, she just couldn't face it. Finally, she explained it this way.

"You see, Dr. Schwartz, my husband and I both came from the same small town. Our families know each other but aren't close. I simply can't break my parents' hearts by admitting failure. I know it would kill them to know of my troubles. I just couldn't face them. So, I've been trying to keep up a good front."

I knew then the real reason for her psychological slavery.

Fortunately, I was able to help her understand that all her parents wanted was for her to be as happy as possible. And, while they wouldn't be happy to learn of her divorce, they certainly would not think ill of her. "Parents like yours," I added, "are much more understanding and much more philosophical than young adults think. Remember," I concluded, "you're not a slave to your husband. Instead you're a slave to your imagined reactions of your parents."

Six months passed before I saw Mrs. J. B. again. She looked excellent, full of life.

"Dr. Schwartz," she said, "I just had to stop by to tell you how things worked out. Guess what my dad said. He said, 'Making a mistake in the first place wasn't nearly as bad as not doing something to correct it.' "

It was obvious to me that Mrs. J. B. had escaped from her psychological prison.

I've known many young men who've gone into business with their father or father-in-law against their intuition and better judgment. Too often, under these circumstances they feel psychologically trapped. Often, in such cases these young men cause their parents far more displeasure than if they had simply insisted on doing what they wanted to do.

Young people who go to college only because parents went there, people who settle down in their home towns when they really like to live elsewhere, and individuals who live in one section of town when they prefer another are all examples of environmental slaves.

There is only one sure cure for environmental slavery. That is to *make a firm decision to control your environment and not let it control you.*

How to Bury Those Psychological Skeletons

Every day many people commit psychological suicide. These people kill a portion of what we commonly refer to as the conscience. These people use two weapons to murder their psyche. The first weapon is embarrassment, and second is guilt.

Embarrassment comes from doing something your training, education, background, and the so-called mores of society say is wrong. The embarrassment complex is caused by doing anything you feel your friends, your superiors, your subordinates, and others around you will not approve. Thinking "I'm second-rate," "I can't do it," "So-and-so is better than I," "I'm not prepared," "I made a fool of myself,"—these are some of the common ways we commit psychological suicide using the embarrassment complex as the murder weapon.

Now, what is guilt? Guilt comes from doing something you instinctively know is wrong. The guilt complex involves the soul. Lying, cheating, stealing, swindling, faking, hiding, these are the ways we commit psychological murder with the guilt complex.

A guilt complex and the embarrassment complex create the same effect. They both inhibit our action, destroy our confidence, create worry, and make us do things in a fearful manner.

Both complexes, guilt and embarrassment, are just as destructive of psychological tissue as cancer is of biological tissue. We cannot do things which we know are wrong and not pay the consequences. Nor can we live with the feeling that we are embarrassed and let our true inner psychic power show through.

Now, make no mistake about this. *You cannot hide an embarrassment complex nor can you hide a guilt complex.* Both show through in essentially the same ways—the inability to look someone in the eye is one common example. Another is found in the weak, quivering, or nervous voice. The body *always* physically shows what the mind is thinking.

These two psychic murder weapons in combination account for the vast majority of pill sales today. Embarrassment, guilt, inferiority, all of these things press so hard on the body that headaches, backaches, indigestion, constipation, and the great variety of minor body ailments all result. For example, as you watch the television commercial you are advised to take a certain pill for constipation. It will bring relief. But what caused the difficulty in the first place? Chances are it is the result of frustration created by one of the two psychic murder weapons, embarrassment or guilt.

Destruction of these two murder weapons is of critical importance to you as you expand and strengthen your ego. Let's see how.

Skeletons can cover any phase of human behavior. For example, here are some common skeletons, and remember as you look at these how much worry and frustration they cause the individual who is trying to keep them locked in the closet.

1. Husband or wife is an alcoholic.
2. Husband or wife is carrying on an affair with another person.
3. Member of the family, perhaps the husband or father, has a police record or is in jail.
4. Teenage daughter is pregnant and unmarried.
5. Young child fails to be admitted to a special prestige school.
6. Individual was fired from previous job.
7. Family has little money and wants to pretend that it has quite a bit.
8. Member of family is undergoing psychiatric treatment or is institutionalized for mental illness.
9. Child is expelled from school for improper behavior.
10. Individual is ashamed of lowly background.

The above list covers just a few of the more common psychological skeletons. A psychological skeleton is anything in your past that you feel is disgraceful or painfully embarrassing. It's the type thing you don't want your friends and associates to know about.

Our society tells us that certain things are "right" and other things are "wrong." We worry about our imperfections, we worry about doing something which is contrary to the code society has established.

Now, of course, none of us is perfect. We fear that if other people know about the skeleton, they will think less of us. So, we go to various extremes to hide the skeleton, keeping it in a mental closet, hoping that no one will find out.

Here are three things you can do to handle skeletons when they come up.

1. *Stop trying to hide skeletons.* My point here is that you don't have to go around wearing a sign saying, "My husband is in jail," or "My wife is an alcoholic," or "I got fired for embezzling on my last job." But what I am suggesting is that when you go to any extreme to cover up something which is embarrassing to you, you are certain to create more mental havoc than you prevent.

One of Atlanta's most respected and acclaimed bankers is a case in point. Mr. B. W. was fired from his job as the Number Two man in a major bank about fifteen years ago for chronic alcoholism—the two-fifths a day variety. But B. W. found himself, took command of his psyche and completely cured himself of alcoholism and any desire for booze. B. W. is now a top official in another bank.

Does he try to keep his past—his psychological skeleton—a secret? Quite the contrary. I've heard B. W. lecture a number of times before large groups of people on the Dangers of Alcoholism in which he uses his own life as a case in point. No one can gossip about B. W. for everyone knows his past.

2. *Remember, your skeletons are as common as sands in the ocean.* All of us are guilty of thinking we are highly unique individuals and that our problems are not very common. The truth is that the skeletons you may be keeping locked in a mental closet are exceedingly common. No one has any right to poke malicious humor at you because of some skeleton for it could be poked to him to just as great a degree.

There is a story told about a woman who had acquired a measure of wealth and, for prestige reasons, wanted to have her family tree traced back two hundred years. She was very status-minded and felt that it would add a great deal to her social position if she could establish her family as being of true blue blood.

So, she hired an expert in this field to find out who her great grandparents and great-great grandparents were. But lo and behold! The expert found that her great grandfather had died in the electric chair for having committed a combination rape and murder. The expert discussed this delicate matter with the rich lady.

Now the lady, I should add, was also a very "honest" woman and not one to lie. She wanted the family tree to reflect the "truth." So, the expert conceived this way out. Rather than write that great grandfather died in an electric chair, he wrote instead, "Great grandfather Jones died while occupying the Chair of Applied Electricity in one of the nation's great institutions."

Now all of us would like to have perfect reputations. All of us would like to come from families who have been nothing but kings, queens, presidents, secretaries of state, philanthropists, etc. But this cannot be.

Let's take time out right now to have a little fun. Let's try to answer the question, "How many relatives do you have?" Make one assumption. Assume it takes 25 years for a generation.

Now, go back 25 years giving or taking a few, and you find you have two parents. Go back 50 years and you have 6 parents —2 parents and 4 grandparents. Go back 75 years and you've got 16 great-grandparents. If you are still with me, go back 100 years and WOW, you have 32 great-grandparents! In other words, every 25 years you go back in time, you double the number of grandparents.

If all of your grandparents since 1725 were assembled, they would number around 500, enough to fill a medium-size convention hall. But watch what happens now. Go back until the time the Pilgrims landed and you'll find you have over 8,000 grandparents. Continue with your multiplication to the time when Columbus discovered America in 1492, and you have 125,000 grandmothers and 125,000 grandfathers for a total of more than a quarter million.

Perhaps we should stop here because the number of your

grandparents is getting too large to handle. Traced back to the year 1300 they would number roughly forty million. And if you went back to the time of the Norman Conquest around 1000 A.D. you'd discover you would have billions of grandparents, more than the total population of the world today.

This brief game in mental gymnastics should convince us of two things. It is certainly true that your family in the broad, long-range concept can boast of relatives who were rich, great military heroes, leading statesmen, explorers, scientists, professors, and generally great individuals.

But likewise, every individual can look back and find that he has ancestors who were murderers, traitors, cowards, cheats, and just plain no-goods.

Perhaps you won't like to know this, but it is just as true as life itself—you are related, literally related, to every person on earth.

Shame, embarrassment, feeling guilty all seem to disappear when we realize that each of us, rich or poor, smart or stupid, handsome or ugly, came from the same biological seed.

Now, let's return from our philosophical digression. Let's go down the street where you live. It makes no difference which house you pick. The family in it has its share of skeletons. For example, one of the skeletons we try hardest to hide is "marital problems." You think because you fight with your wife or husband that this is unique, something which you have got to hide at all costs, something for which you must carry an artificial front, and thereby avoid detection.

But I've got news for you. Marital problems are so bad that divorce is the ultimate result in one-third of our families. Now, at least another third of the families have such severe problems that they contemplate divorce. And the remaining one-third of the couples are not exactly getting along in a state of pure bliss!

Again, remember other people have their own skeletons and actually haven't got time to be thinking about yours. Your problems, your skeletons, are not unique.

3. *Stop depositing bad thoughts in your memory bank.* In many ways your brain can be compared with a bank. You deposit money in the bank or you take money out. The same deposit and withdrawal process takes place in your brain. You deposit thoughts and you withdraw thoughts.

Now, one of the ways we commit psychological suicide is to withdraw negative thoughts from our memory bank and put these in our mental billfold. Then, as we go about our work spending our thoughts, we find we are spending negatives instead of positives. The result helps lead to psychic suicide.

Each of us has a memory bank. And it's a big one. Think of it, everything that has ever happened to you is stored away in that memory vault. Ever notice how as you grow older you remember things which you had forgotten for many years? This simply shows that every event in the past still lives in your memory. We read a lot these days about computers. But a dozen computers can't store as much information as one human brain. Truly you own a fantastic bank.

A thing to bear in mind here is that you and only you have the keys to this memory bank. Only you can decide what you will remember.

While you can't always decide what you are going to withdraw from your memory bank, you have complete control as to how to interpret that memory. Thanks to the unique nature of the human mind you have the power to interpret a memory as either positive or negative.

The same memory will rock one person but amuse another simply because each of us chooses to remember in our own way.

What's the point? Choose to recall a memory positively. Learn to laugh at your defeats. Learn to recall it as a lesson, but never look upon it as negative.

Expand the famous quotation, "All things work together for good," to "All things can be *remembered* for good."

4. *You can't go wrong when you do what's right.* Not long ago I was going over a bibliography of books written on "How to

Hire Personnel." Mind you, there have been over 350 books written that tell you how to do a good job of selecting people to work for you.

But let's turn this question around. How many books are there which tell you how to remove someone from a job? How many books tell us how to fire someone?

Right here is where a lot of executives I know experience guilt. I have seen many executives and many people in management worry a great deal about their task of having to dismiss someone. Many people, of course, live a lifetime without having to face a decision of this kind. But it is impossible for anyone to rise very far in the business and professional world without having to perform this task. Every week, for example, an estimated 100,000 people are involuntarily terminated from their jobs. And these people are at all levels, ranging from unskilled laborers to senior executives.

An executive told me just recently, "I'll feel terrible if I have to remove that woman from her job. After all she is sixty years old and she can't find another. It's true that she can't get along with the people at work, but I just can't bear to have her hardship on my conscience."

We established that there was no other economic alternative to follow. She could not be transferred to another division. She could not be given a different job. The only practical alternative was to remove her from her job. But the executive claimed he could not.

The only question that must be answered here is, "Is the welfare of the organization more important than the welfare of any individual?" If the answer is "Yes," then you have no choice. Then too, we must remember that keeping an inefficient individual on a job is working hardships on other people and is denying someone else a chance to get started. This is a round-about way of saying, "You can't go wrong doing what's right."

During the war it was necessary for tens of thousands of Americans to kill the enemy through all forms of personal and impersonal forms of destruction. It would be foolish, of course, to think that an individual who killed an enemy should feel guilty about having done so. The objective was—win the war. Winning the war was right. Therefore, you couldn't go wrong in carrying out those assignments necessary to win the war.

I don't think I've ever heard of a surgeon who honestly enjoyed amputations. No surgeon likes to amputate a leg on a young lady or a young man. But should he feel guilty or should he lie awake at night thinking he has done a wrong?

The answer, of course, is no. He removes the leg for only one reason—so the rest of the body can live. Granted it is better to have two legs than one, but it's also better to have one leg and be alive than two legs and be dead.

Often it does take a lot of psychological guts to do what's right. Much of the indecision in life (and indecision is one of the great causes of psychic suicide) can be traced to an inability to understand the concept, "You can't go wrong doing what is right."

WRITE YOUR OWN PSYCHOLOGICAL EMANCIPATION PROCLAMATION

The only free people today are those who choose *to be free. Why not join them? Just:*

1. Conquer "other people" slavery. Remember, "other people" are followers, not leaders. You're nobody until you are criticized for what you do.

2. Respect your ability, your intelligence, your opinions. Develop a favorable self-image.

3. Stop thinking you're too old. Age is mainly a state of mind.

4. Learn to like living dangerously. Enjoy the fact you don't know for sure what will happen tomorrow.

5. Regard your losses as part of your education. Remember, winning is a state of mind.

6. Change your environment if you don't like it.

7. Bury those psychological skeletons—
. . . stop trying to hide them

...*remember, your skeletons are as common as sands in the ocean*

...*stop depositing bad thoughts in your memory bank*

...*bear in mind, you can't go wrong doing what is right.*

How To Use
Psychic Power
To Gain Help
From Others

3

Now it's time to deal *directly* with the classic question all success-conscious people ask. "Is it push or pull?"

"Brains or persuasive power?"

"What I do?" or "Who I know?"

"Pure ability?" or "Sales ability?"

Summed up in two words, it's the human touch that does it. This human touch is the spark—the atomic reactor of people-persuasion that gets people to do things for you willingly and gladly.

The best way to learn this lesson is watch a rocket take off. How does it get up there and go into orbit? The rocket is literally lifted off. (That's why they call it "lift off.")

Now, are you pulled up or lifted up? Is there someone reaching down throwing you a rope and then pulling you up? Or must you be lifted to the top? And if it's lift, who supplies it?

Now, does pull exert some effect on the rocket? Yes, but only after it's far up. Same thing holds true in business. Pull takes over after a heck of a lot of thrust is exerted.

The lift is determined by your ability to get people to *support* you, *work* for you, *sacrifice* for you, *do favors* for you, *help* you, *buy* from you, *sell* for you. That's what lift is. Now, how do we get it?

Take Two Men	Intelligence Quotient	Likability Quotient
Fred	125	100
Bill	100	125

Chances are, Bill will greatly outdistance Fred. In this age, the likability quotient is more highly rewarded than the intelligence quotient.

It's wonderful, of course, if we have both—the high intelligence quotient and the high likability quotient.

But knowing something about you (the fact you are reading this) is proof you've got enough native intelligence to go any distance you desire. Lack of brains can never be your excuse.

The ability to get other people to lift you is an absolute requirement to achieve the degree of success you want. President Lyndon Johnson learned this a long time ago. To help himself develop persuasive power, he developed ten personal rules for motivating people. Study them carefully.

PRESIDENT JOHNSON'S 10 RULES FOR MOTIVATING PEOPLE [1]

1. Learn to remember names. Inefficiency at this point may indicate that your interest is not sufficiently outgoing.

2. Be a comfortable person so there is no strain in being with you. Be an old-shoe, old-hat kind of individual.

3. Acquire the quality of relaxed easy-going so that things do not ruffle you.

---

[1] *The Magic of Thinking Big,* by David J. Schwartz, Prentice-Hall, Inc., Englewood Cliffs, N.J., 1959, page 142.

4. Don't be egotistical. Guard against the impression that you know it all.

5. Cultivate the quality of being interesting so people will get something of value from their association with you.

6. Study to get the "scratchy" elements out of your personality, even those of which you may be unconscious.

7. Sincerely attempt to heal, on an honest Christian basis, every misunderstanding you have had or now have. Drain off your grievances.

8. Practice liking people until you learn to do so genuinely.

9. Never miss an opportunity to say a word of congratulation upon anyone's achievement, or express sympathy in sorrow or disappointment.

10. Give spiritual strength to people, and they will give genuine affection to you.

Learn the Multiplication Tables

To maximize your gains you must be able to multiply your talent through other people. That is, as a leader, you must be able to get others to (a) buy your ideas and orders, and (b) implement them.

I have seen the psychological stall technique used hundreds of times. By this, I mean people are given orders, they pretend to accept them; but then they never quite get down to carrying them out.

One of the most popular Presidents of the U. S. in modern times was Eisenhower. And the slogan, which best described *why* he was so popular and so effective was simply, "We Like Ike."

An officer in the navy once explained something very important to me. "If you have to wear a gold stripe to win respect and get follow-through on your orders, then you aren't fit to wear the stripe," he said. "If you have to have gold bars to exercise authority, then you don't deserve the bars." If this is true in the service, then think how much truer it is in business where you don't have gold bars.

Leadership is not simply a matter of gold bars, of symbols or positions of authority. A position of leadership alone does not make an effective leader. What does make a leader is the golden touch, the ability to handle people.

Surprisingly few people have the golden touch. But it's easy to develop if you master five rules. Master them and you've gone a long way toward mastering your psychic power.

1. Show your human side. It counts most.
2. Give—and when it's not expected.
3. Make people you want to influence feel needed.
4. Equate yourself with people at *their* level.
5. Keep secrets secret.

Show Your Human Side. It Counts Most

Recently I had a chat with a close physician friend of mine who has one of those standing-room-only practices in a suburban community. I asked him to explain why some doctors are so much busier than others.

He smiled, thought a few seconds then said, "I think it comes down to this. To build a large loyal practice you've got to care about people—to treat each one like his ailment or problem is the most important thing in the world.

"I'm often secretly amused," he went on, "when a new patient comes to me and says 'a friend told me you're the best doctor around.' I do feel I'm a good doctor, but I don't believe that I can do a better job of treating tonsilitis or chicken pox or the other common illnesses than a dozen other doctors on this side of town.

"And besides," the doctor added, "I can't say this to everyone, but the truth is the average layman isn't qualified to judge doctors. Medical competency is exceptionally difficult to determine.

"I think I have a large practice because I like people. For example, I've made it a rule never to belittle a person who thinks there is something wrong with her when physically there isn't. She has a problem and I listen sympathetically and try to help. In this profession you must have consideration for people in addition to medical knowledge."

The human, the I-like-you attitude makes the difference in other pursuits too. One of the top merchandising executives of a clothing chain gave his views on competition with small stores this way:

"Little stores can't beat us on price—we buy direct and in larger quantity so we get much bigger discounts. And we're way ahead of the small store on variety. We offer customers several times the choice of merchandise. And in most cases we're way out front in modern facilities, lighting, air conditioning and other store conveniences.

"But there is one area in which the small merchant has the edge if he uses it."

"What's that?" I asked.

"Put in one phrase, it's the human touch," he answered. "The small merchant can get to know his customers. He can develop a friendly warmth to his store. And if he does, it erases his disadvantages.

"We are spending a lot of time and money to build a warm personality in each of our stores. If you haven't got that, you simply aren't as successful as you could be."

Imagine: the I-like-you attitude even makes the difference in modern-day retailing.

People are more interested in the human side of you than in your possessions, or positions, or salary. This was driven home to me several years ago by a prominent speaker whom I was asked to introduce to a large audience.

Prior to the introduction the speaker drew me aside and said, "Will you do me a favor? When you introduce me play down my education, business connections, and all that other stuffy information. I want to get the audience warm to me at the very start.

3

Here's a card with some things I'd appreciate your telling the audience." The card said:

1. Your speaker has five beautiful daughters who are an assortment of blondes, brunettes, and redheads. And he's keeping them locked up away from people like you.

2. Served in the Pacific during World War II as an Air Inspector—and all he inspected was air.

3. Never touches a golf ball but works out three times weekly lifting weights. His personal goal is to be the world's strongest man.

4. Closed the biggest business deal of his life in a hospital bed —and he didn't marry the nurse. He sold 6,000 aluminum windows to a new hospital.

5. Favorite slogan is

   "Early to bed
   Early to rise
   Work like the devil
   And advertise."

After the talk the speaker explained to me that in his experience a man's hobby is more interesting than his executive title or the degrees he holds. People want to know the personal, the human things about other people. Make sure you win acceptance quickly and fully. Be human.

The human side is the interesting side. The reading public is immensely interested in the human side of celebrities. They want to know what they eat for breakfast, where they go for entertainment, the names of their children, all about their romances and so on.

People aren't interested in cold, formal "hard" facts. They want to know you are human.

Rub people the human way and you rub people the right way.

Don't Be Afraid of Sentiment—
It's Power in Disguise

Hard, cruel, steel-eyed people aren't on top. President Lyndon Johnson said in a recent interview, "Show me a man who can't cry when he sees a widowed woman with little children and sores all over their little bodies and I'll show you a fellow who ought not to be in public life."

Some cynics, of course, will tell you that this is corn, that a skilled politician says such things to win votes. But cynics are just jealous soreheads. Even a dog can spot insincerity and it seems unreasonable to believe that someone can pretend to feel sympathetic toward people and not be easily detected. Big people aren't afraid of sentiment. They aren't afraid to cry. And sentiment, a feeling of love and concern for fellow human beings, is a source of power.

Dr. Loren Eiseley, noted anthropologist, made this comment about the civilizing influence of tenderness:

> Man in his arrogance may boast that the battle is to the strong, that pity and affection are signs of weakness. Nevertheless, in spite of the widespread popularity of such ideas, the truth is that if man at heart were not a tender creature toward his kind, a loving creature in a peculiarly special way, he would long since have left his bones to the wild dogs that roved the African grasslands where he first essayed the great adventure of becoming human.[2]

"Oh, don't be sentimental," is some of the worst advice you have ever received. Being sentimental, feeling for other people gives your soul a chance to work with you.

Remember: Don't be afraid of sentiment.

---

[2] *Saturday Evening Post*, April 26, 1958.

Ask: Am I Doing It the Human Way?

Below are some practice exercises to make you more human—and thereby more popular and influential. Put them to use.

HUMANIZE EVERYTHING YOU DO

Situation	How
1. Writing a letter	Write it so it sounds as if you were talking with him. Avoid the impersonal, "This is to advise you" tone. Make some statement that shows you think of him as a person. Something like, "I really enjoyed our last conversation. I've given a lot of thought to what you said, especially your comment about. . . ." "I've got some good news for you."
2. Your handshake	Shake hands like you really *are* glad to see the other person. Make it warm, firm. Make it enthusiastic. Don't convey the impression, "I'm used to shaking lots of hands, this is pure routine."
3. Giving advice to a subordinate	Let the other person know you're human—that you had the same problem once. Let him know you are interested in his personal success. "John, believe me, the only reason I mention this small point is because I want to see you climb higher fast."
4. Introducing a speaker	Finding something "human" to say about him—something in which he takes much personal pride—his family, hobbies, ideas. Don't overdo the factual statements of previous jobs, present job, memberships, and so on.

5. Your smile   When you smile, *smile*. Mean it. A half-hearted smile is almost as bad as a frown.

Several weeks ago I visited an executive friend who was in the hospital for two weeks following an operation. During my visit I remarked about the numerous floral bouquets in his room.

"There are a lot of them and I've also received a lot of cards. I appreciate them. But in a way they annoy me a trifle."

"Why?" I asked.

"Well," he went on, "too much card sending and flower sending is routine these days. I know because I'm guilty of it myself. I can just visualize an executive telling his secretary, 'See that Bill Jones gets some flowers. I believe he's at the Piedmont but you'd better check. Spend ten—no, better make it a $20 piece. He's a pretty good customer.'

"The remembrances that make the biggest impression on me are personal notes, something that shows they care enough about me to go to a little extra trouble.

"I've resolved this," he went on. "When I get on the outside, I'm going to remember my sick friends with personal notes. I'll still send cards or gifts too, but most important is the personal note. I'll show them they are non-routine friends."

Moral: Humanize it. Personalize it. The impact and positive effect is 1,000 percent greater.

Give and Give When It Isn't Expected

I'll make a bet with you. I'll bet you can't find a generous person who isn't well-liked. And I'll make another bet with you. I'll wager you can't find a tight, selfish individual who is well-liked. Likability always follows generosity! This is an amazing thing. And what is equally amazing is that people who are generous, people who give, are those who get and get and get!

I know a successful realtor who owns and manages three

large office buildings. Most real estate people give something to their tenants at Christmas time. They generally give a fifth or two of booze.

My friend operates differently. He keeps in mind that his tenants are individuals. He has given many unusual gifts, which by the way, generally cost very little.

One time I asked him, "Sam, do you think your giving pays off?" It didn't take Sam long to reply. "My tenants are the most loyal of any in this town. I never have vacant space. Yet, I charge more per square foot and I don't always have a good space to rent. But they continue to stick with me because I like them."

Then he named a less successful competitor, "Now you take ————. He gives his tenants a gift at Christmas time. That's all.

"But Christmas," he said, "is in my heart all year long. I put it there and I keep it there."

Now, of course, the negative-oriented individual will tell you, "Well, Sam can afford to be generous. After all he's a millionaire." But these people miss the whole point. Sam's generosity is not the result of his riches. Sam's generosity is the *cause* of his riches.

Repeatedly, I've discovered that highly successful people are usually very generous individuals. Let me tell you about my friend, John Gunn. Several months ago, I was scheduled to give a talk in Atlanta and another in a resort area in Tennessee only about ninety minutes apart. This was a mistake in my scheduling, but I did not realize it until it was too late. There were no possible airline connections. So, I knew I would have to charter a plane. Since I was not personally acquainted with charter services, I decided to call my friend, John, and ask him for his opinion inasmuch as I knew that he had his own plane and was quite familiar with the two companies who operated charter services.

I explained my problem to John and asked him which of the two charter services he'd recommend. Without one second's hesitation, he said, "I recommend the 'John Gunn' line." I felt this was a tremendous imposition and tried to beg out of it but he would not hear of it. So, my friend flew me to the site. Now here was an example of an individual who expected nothing in return.

But expecting nothing in return is the finest way to give. My friend, Gunn, is continually doing the hard thing. He gives the hard-to-get football ticket. He always is picking up special gifts in far-away places for his friends.

Is it paying off? It sure is. John has developed one of the finest businesses of its kind in the nation. His generosity is one of the chief ingredients of his success. John gives and John gets—*more*.

It's very natural—and very desirable—to want to get. But what is not so natural is the upside-down way most people seem to approach the goal of getting.

Most people commit this error: they think, "What can he do for me?" instead of thinking, "What can I do for him?"

The difference between these two thought patterns is the difference between being mediocre and being highly successful.

It seems odd but it is correct. *Put giving first and getting takes care of itself.* The generous prosper. The selfish don't. You can rely on this as a general rule: *Prosperity varies in proportion to generosity.*

Make People You Want to Influence Feel Needed

A professional psychologist recently gave me his views on what is behind many teenage problems and teenage misbehavior.

"Many young people today feel left out of the family circle," he explained. In many homes, the teenager is made to feel like the fourth string end on the football team. He doesn't get a chance to play in the family game. Teenagers have a tremendous capacity to show interest. But if they can't identify themselves with the family's course—with its goals—then they devote all of their attention to situations where they feel useful and appreciated."

"Smart parents," he went on, "give their children something to do, something to make them feel useful. Children want to feel they are more than caged pets."

This point of view makes sense, doesn't it? People in any

situation lose interest—and lose it fast—when they are made to feel useless. I recall a minister telling me about one of his Sunday School teachers who had broken all records for building class attendance.

"Mort [the successful teacher] took over a particularly difficult class. There were only four or five regular members. But a year later, class attendance averaged 22," the minister began.

I was very curious as to how this teacher could accomplish so much. I commented to the minister, "Mort must really be a great teacher to develop such attendance."

The minister half smiled and with a wink said, "Mort's a fine teacher. He knows what he talks about. But equally important, Mort's a *smart* teacher. As soon as he took over the class he immediately found something for each member to do. He made each class member feel that he depended on him, that the class couldn't function without him. And because they felt needed and useful, old members and new members became regular members."

The simple technique of making people feel "needed and useful" built a Sunday School class from 4 to 22 in a single year!

Often, for no apparent reason, my mind thinks of the late Dr. H. H. Maynard, one of the finest professors I was ever privileged to know. Dr. Maynard taught me many things but perhaps the most significant lesson I learned from him occurred when I had just finished an intensified course of study under his direction.

I had learned of what was a "terrific" job. The job called for a more experienced person than I and one with more ability than I thought I had. Still, I wanted that job. Something inside me and all over me said, "Dave, this one should be for you. You can handle it."

I knew that one person and one person only could help me get that job. That person was H. H. Maynard. Because of his unusually outstanding reputation, I could have that job if he simply "put in a good word for me."

But I hesitated. I knew Dr. Maynard, like all great men, was not easy with his words of praise. Finally, the desire to win that job had so thoroughly absorbed me that I had no choice but to ask Dr. Maynard for his help. To my surprise, Dr. Maynard was delighted to help. "I was hoping you'd call on me for a little help. I would have been hurt if you had not."

Right then is when I learned the great lesson. People *do* want to help you!

Now, many years later, I, too, find myself very eager to help deserving students win those "terrific jobs."

All of us want to feel needed and useful.

Mrs. Ruth Barbee, a marriage consultant who has helped many couples discover the truly deep joys of married life, recently said this about reviving romance: "The best advice I can give any woman is always to remember that a man must feel a woman *needs* him." [3]

And the point can be made in reverse. A woman must feel that a man *needs* her. Many, many, conscientious, hard-working husbands miss out on much affection at home because they give their wives just about everything except that "I need you" feeling. A physician acquaintance had just this problem. Here's how he explained it: "Ellen and I married while I was still a pre-med student. I had almost no income so the only way I could continue in school was for Ellen to work. But Ellen didn't mind at all. Looking back, those were wonderful years. We both felt we were working together for a common purpose. Well, after four years, I started practicing and it was possible for Ellen to give up her job. We had to watch the dollars pretty close for a while, but my practice developed rapidly and money ceased to be a problem.

"But the odd thing," the doctor went on, "the more money I made, the farther we seemed to drift apart. Neither of us had any reason to suspect that the other had been attracted by someone else—nothing like that. Rather, it was more like a feeling of growing indifference. There were no quarrels, no loud fusses. It was even worse. Our marriage had become a 'ho hum' arrangement.

"Finally on a long overdue vacation we had a long, long, talk and I learned what a fool I had been."

---

[3] As reported in the *Atlanta Journal*, February 12, 1959.

"What do you mean?" I asked.

"After a lot of talk, mostly on my part, I asked that question all pig-headed husbands ask, 'Haven't I given you everything you want?' This really mixed up Ellen's emotions and she began crying and said, 'When we were first married you needed me. You depended on me. Now you don't. Now you are totally self-sufficient. Why don't you let me help you once in a while? Why don't you make me feel like I'm needed?'

"That really jolted me. It was true. For the past fifteen years, I had done everything money could do to make life easy for Ellen. I had even moved into a separate bedroom so the occasional night phone call wouldn't wake her. I had given her everything possible except the chance for her to help me."

At that point I couldn't help but rush the conversation with, "Well, what did you do then?"

"Really it was quite simple. Ellen confessed a little later that she wanted to help out in my office. This sort of took me back because I had the foolish notion that my wife in the office would suggest that my income is slipping. But I gave in and I'm glad I did. Ellen is as bright and happy as when we first met."

You can put the "make people feel needed" principle to work for you in many big and little situations. A friend told he how he used this technique to get to know his neighbors and make friends with them. "When we moved into the community no one went out of their way to get to know us. But we don't like it that way. We realized it was really our place to introduce ourselves first. So I devised this plan to break the ice with our cold neighbors. I suggested to my wife that she borrow something from each neighbor the next week—anything—a little coffee, soap, flour, etc.

"This gave her two chances to meet them—once to borrow and once to pay back. And it opened the door to friendship. People love to do little favors for you. Give them that chance."

Remember: It is better to give than to receive. Letting someone else do something for you often does much more to win a friend than your doing something for him.

The "make people feel needed approach" can be used in any

situation in which other people are involved. Salesmen can use it by asking customers to recommend prospects. It's surprising how glad customers are to help the appreciative salesman expand business. Teachers can motivate students by asking students to help out with minor but necessary tasks. When I was a youngster in school, we felt mighty important when the teacher asked us to dust the erasers or do some other little task.

Now, in the college classroom I traditionally appoint two students to serve as "unofficial assistants." They check rolls, run errands and do many small but important things.

How to Put the "Make People Feel Needed" Technique to Work

Remember this basic truth: People *want* to feel needed. They *want* to help. They *want* to feel they are a part of you and what you do. Satisfy this want and receive admiration, respect, loyalty, and cooperation in return.

Skilled camp directors make certain each person has some definite responsibility. Skilled performers bring people in on the act. Recently I witnessed an interesting night club act in which the fellow on stage made a terrific hit—not because he was so good—I and the people with me couldn't judge that—but because he had everybody in the audience singing, shaking hands, doing something.

Recently, a young man explained to me how he put the "Let people help you" principle to work. "I wanted desperately to move up fast in my company," he explained. "I was going to college while I worked. But I felt completely unrecognized in the company. One day I decided I would try to see the vice-president in charge of my division and ask him if he would help me plan the remainder of my college program. I explained that I had every intention of staying on after I finished school and I wanted to get the best possible preparation. Well, I saw the company vice-president and he was indeed impressed. He told me that he had done a great variety of things for employees but this was the first time this had happened. He was really excited. He asked me to come in at the end of every quarter and report on my progress.

"The end result was that I became sort of a special project. I had put him on my side by letting him in on my educational program."

I've made this same recommendation—get the other fellow in on the act—many times for dozens of situations. It works. Successful salesmen use this technique to sell difficult prospects.

Get the top to feel you are a special project—someone to help, coach, develop. This is a law of influence. When people are left out, they are indifferent, when they feel left out on purpose, they become opposition.

Tension in business situations often runs high. Big men are hard to sell. But a friend of mine, Joe Wilson, who is in charge of a new business for a large advertising agency, has a method. Joe is in charge of preparing the presentations to use in attempting to sell new accounts. Normally, the fellow in charge of the activity really is on the spot. There are radio and television experts who are tough to please; there are newspaper experts, research experts, all with their own ideas.

But Joe has a method that prevents friction. As he builds his presentation he invites other executives to look it over individually. Then he incorporates a few of their suggestions. Finally, when the presentation is ready to go, all the men have been in on the preliminary work and are already sold. Joe has made them feel part of the team. And they love and support him for it.

If you want something from someone else—his approval, his order, his okay, his acceptance—then get him in on the act early.

There's an old story passed among sales executives that tells how a thoroughly experienced salesman doubled orders for cash registers. He would visit the new prospect, introduce himself, then say something like, "Mr. Brown, I didn't come here to sell you a machine. I came here to get some advice. I'm new at this and I wonder if you'd show me how I ought to sell it." Almost invariably the prospect, being intensely complimented, would work up an enthusiastic sales presentation. After this the salesman would say, "You make it sound like you need one." And many sales resulted just by letting the other fellow take part.

Make it a personal resolution to let your associates, customers, children, husband or wife,—anyone you live close to—feel you need them.

Just two don'ts:

1. Don't, of course, be overbearing. Don't ask them to do especially difficult things for you.

2. Don't fail to show sincere appreciation. People want to help—and will continue to want to help you—only if they feel you truly are grateful.

Equate Yourself with other People

Once while visiting in a small southern town I happened to hear a young politician—one of the "new" breed—make a political speech. It was a hot August day and the audience was not particularly enthusiastic. The candidate spent most of his time talking about international trade, reciprocity, and similar topics.

Finally he finished. After the polite but mild applause, I turned to the old-timer who had been leaning against the same telephone pole as I, and asked, "Well, what do you think of that speech?"

The rugged fellow who obviously was a man of few words replied, "I don't reckon I understood it. I always figure a guy who can't talk plain talk ain't got no business talking."

I will remember always that observation—"A guy who can't talk plain talk ain't got no business talking"—as one of the most significant lessons I've learned from anyone anywhere.

You simply can't hold attention with anything less than plain talk. Anyone who has ever sat in on presentations by advertising agencies to large advertisers appreciates this. The presentations made to highly intelligent businessmen are simple.

"To be simple," said Emerson, "is to be great."

One frequently hears comments about the average intelligence of people. These remarks refer to the mind of the 13 year old or the 12 year old. A good rule, I believe, is to make it simple enough for a seven year old to understand. I learned something about this in trying to explain things to my son. He would ask me questions such as, "What does profit mean?" or, "Dad, what does efficiency mean?" I would try to explain. And I'd keep trying until it was quite obvious that he understood. And I've learned this too. The same definitions that he could understand were also the ones most understandable to college seniors!

I confess what I've learned about space comes more from Walt Disney films and top grade comics than from scientific reports. Walt Disney Studios has developed the ability to take vastly complex things and make them simple. Of course, some say, "Well, it's my job to tell them and it's their job to understand." Look—the most intelligent people in the country will go to sleep on you if you say things they can't understand.

Something is lacking in your communicative skill if the basic essentials of what you say can't be understood by a child. Attention given you is in direct proportion to how well what you say is comprehended. Making things simple increases comprehension. Therefore, simplicity increases attention. And attention is what you must have if you are going to influence other people.

I have many friends in the hill country. And one of the things I admire most about them is their ability to use words for maximum value. Their supply of tools (words) is generally short; but they compensate for this by using their tool chest effectively. The trouble with some so-called educated people is that they go around using some expensive tool when a plain old 25¢ pliers would do the job—and better.

Only a very small fraction of what is said and written is understood. And this is not because the average guy is dumb or under-educated. No. No. No! I've seen executives with I.Q.'s of 130 and better fall asleep during speeches. I've seen people with I.Q.'s below 90 who are attentive, wide-awake.

The burden for holding attention falls on you.

If something is over their heads, don't think they are stupid. Be big enough to realize that you simply haven't made it simple enough for them to understand.

The biggest battle in communications you fight in this world can be summed up in two words, "get attention." There's enormous competition for it. And attention goes to the thing most easily understood. Attention fights complexity.

Use words that are alive, expressive, and above all, understood. Use words that create vivid mind pictures. When you use dull words or oversized words or confusing words, you create the wrong image of you in the minds of the people you're talking to. The image may be one of these:

1. He's a stuffed shirt—a show off.
2. He doesn't understand what he's talking about.
3. I'm indifferent to him.
4. He bores me.

Attention is so easily lost. Remember, when you talk to a person you are talking to someone who has literally tens of millions of memories stashed inside his cranium. He may recall one or a series of these rather than digest what you are saying. People who speak a great deal know how easily attention can drift away.

The big problem here is to realize that the world doesn't pay any attention at all to things it doesn't understand.

Here's the way to remember it: *Always put the fodder down there where the calves can eat it.* I've heard this same principle referred to as the KISS technique (Keep it simple, stupid).

Remember, as you talk you may have the other person's body, but you don't necessarily have his mind. It is easy for a person sitting across the table from you to wander off to Japan, Europe, go back home, go a thousand places and still be physically in the room with you. That's why holding attention is so important.

Use Examples to Clarify What You Say

Some years ago in Lincoln, Nebraska, I happened to hear two ministers deliver sermons within just a few months of each other on the general topic of "Eternity—How Long Is It?" In both cases the objective was to help people realize eternity is a long time and it's important to be prepared.

Well, the first minister got up and with much emphasis explained that "Eternity is forever. Yes, my friend, eternity is forever." Despite his continued reference to "eternity is forever," the congregation was not very impressed.

The second sermon on "Eternity—How Long Is It?" developed many times the interest in the audience. The second minister proceeded to help the congregation visualize how long eternity is with an illustration. His story went something like this: "Imagine a steel tower 10 miles on each side and 100 miles high placed at the North Pole. Once each year a small bird flies to this tower to sharpen his little beak. Well, when this tower of steel has been worn away from the bird's beak-sharpening—then that will be just one minute in eternity." The example this minister used made eternity a lot longer than a mere "forever."

The point here is translate a concept into something people can grasp. The ability to be understood is the greatest ability of all.

Note as you listen to influential people how they use examples to illustrate points they wish to make. The most influential person in history—Jesus—used parables to illustrate the concepts he wanted people to accept. He did not just tell people, "Do this and do that." Rather, he showed with examples why it is best to do this and do that.

People give their attention to a good storyteller—someone who can make a point with an example of people.

Keep Secrets Secret

A physician in a small town had built a good practice. But he lacked one of the important ingredients of being a professional —he discussed one patient's medical problem with another. This hurt. While many people are eager to learn what's "really" wrong with someone else, they, in turn, want to be sure that their ailments are not discussed.

Keep secrets secret. This takes some doing. There is a natural ache to pass on secrets. Every day you hear conversations like this: "I just heard—and please keep this secret—that so and so is being such and such." Few, very few, people can keep confidences.

This fact has several implications for you. For one thing it means be extra careful in confiding in other people. Don't confide unless you are really sure the confidence will be kept.

But equally important, the ability—and it is an ability—to keep secrets is one of the primary ways to win influence over other people. Develop your ability to keep matters confidential and you win two ways.

First, you win friends. Other people will become tremendously devoted to you when they know what they tell you stops right there.

Second, you become better informed. You'll know what is going on so you'll be able to make better plans.

But suppose you know some confidential information and a close friend asks you what you know. What should you do then? Just this. Say something like this, "I appreciate your interest in Jack, but the person who gave me the information asked that I keep it confidential." Jack will appreciate your integrity and won't press you further. Jack will see that rare quality of keeping secrets secret.

People violate the confidence rule in another way. They don't tell the confidential information directly. But they give you so many clues, it's like trying to identify the *Star Spangled Banner* after hearing six or eight bars. This is just as bad as spreading information directly.

Loyalty comes to you in proportion to your ability to keep confidences.

A college president explained one of his administrative techniques. "You'd be surprised how many people get in trouble. They come to me with their troubles and I help them. They aren't afraid to talk because they know what's said here remains here."

Remember the Ripple Effect When
You Talk with People

Let's suppose you sit down and talk with someone—let's call him Mr. A.—about a juicy bit of gossip. Within minutes or hours some or all of what you said will be resaid by Mr. A. to Mr. B., Mr. C., and Mr. D. Mr. B. tells E., F., and G.; C tells H., I., and J.; and D. tells K., L., and M. Word travels in geometric progression. Like ripples in a quiet lake, news travels far and fast.

Leaders are quite aware of this fact. As one president of a medium-sized company explained it to me, "Three or four people, other than my staff, will see me each morning. But by 1 A.M. virtually everyone in the organization has heard the high points of our discussion. The coffee break will start much of the news going and the lunch hour will take care of the rest. I've learned this. When I talk to one person, it's the same as talking to 200 more. Everybody is a reporter."

The fact that just about everyone is a reporter doesn't mean you must be an icy, tight-lipped Mr. "No Comment." If you are, your chances for leadership are killed because leaders are expected to talk. The objective is not say nothing. Rather, the objective is to say things that you would like to see resaid. When someone talks to you, think beyond this immediate conversation to the one that will take place next. Practice these rules:

1. Say things that you want resaid.
2. Pass out helpful, positive, encouraging news.

And remember, what you say will be resaid in different form. If you say something negative, it will be far more negative after having been resaid five times. Vice versa. Say something positive and it will grow more positive through repetition.

Speak with discretion. Say things you want resaid with your label. Ask yourself, "Would I say this to 100 people?" before you say it.

NOW, GET BUSY DEVELOPING YOUR GOLDEN TOUCH

Just ...

1. Decide to develop your likability quotient.

2. Show your human side in everything you do. Avoid being cold, cruel, and calculating.

3. Give to Get. Remember, put giving first and getting takes care of itself. Prosperity varies in proportion to generosity.

4. Make people around you feel needed. Ask people to help you, do favors for you. It's an excellent way to make them feel useful.

5. Equate yourself with people you want to influence. Talk on their level. Trade minds with people you want to influence.

6. Keep secrets secret. Become a confidant to people around you and you win their devotion and respect.

How To Stop
Worrying
And Start Living
Again

4

Let me tell you about a continuing psychic probe I've been conducting now for five years. The results will surprise you. They are almost unbelievable. Yet they are true and exceedingly significant to those of us who want to climb on top and achieve peace of mind.

The experiment is this: I've been asking people (in private conferences and in group discussions) to tell me in complete confidence what they worry about. To date I've tabulated the worries of over 2500 individuals.

Now, the most amazing result of this study is what people *don't* worry about. Get this: I have yet to find one person who mentioned "Fear of nuclear attack" as one of his worries. Each of these 2500 people admitted he loses sleep over worries. But not one of these thousands of people has lost any sleep worrying about the big bomb.

Now, logic would tell you that if we are going to worry, the big bomb should be near the top of our worry list. It is estimated that there is enough nuclear potency available right now to kill everyone on earth 12 times and more is being manufactured every day! But fear of radio-active cremation isn't even important enough to mention when people start naming their worries! We're spending billions every year to protect us from something we do not fear.

Here's another discovery that helps us put worry in true perspective. Only a very few of these people mentioned "Being injured or killed in an automobile accident" as a key worry. Yet, if you're looking for something to worry about, this is it. More than 40,000 Americans will die this year in auto crashes and over 3,000,000 will be injured. But do we worry? No. Many of the folks picked up dead after an auto crash hadn't even bothered to fasten their seat belts!

Let me put the worry problem in even sharper focus. I'm thinking now of a 24-year-old, 190 pound, 5 ft. 10 in. man—exceptionally strong, exceptionally powerful—who served as a paratrooper in the army and later took up sky-diving as a hobby. He has the capability of breaking your neck with one swat of his hand. I doubt whether four average men could manage to contain him.

Physical fear? No. This fellow has none. Psychic fear? Well, that's a different story. As a student of mine I gave him an assignment that involved getting up before a group of 20 other students and making a 5 minute oral report. The day before his scheduled talk he came in and confessed he was simply too scared to talk. His fear was so great I had to make an exception in his case and excuse him.

It's amazing, isn't it? No fear of jumping 20,000 feet out of an aircraft but terrible fear of standing for five minutes before a group of unarmed students!

How Our Mind Cripples Our Growth

Here's the point in a nutshell. We worry about psychic dangers, not physical dangers. Our worry is almost exclusively mind —not body.

We worry about love, grades in school, jobs, the neighbors. We worry about our teenage children and what they are doing. We worry about promotion, status, prestige. We worry about customers that won't buy and creditors that won't pay. We worry about things of the mind.

Now to make things even worse, worries breed worries. Just consider the mathematics of worry in this example.

Jim Brown is a salesman, 35 years old, two youngsters in school. Jim lives in a modest home, is doing a reasonably good job but runs scared. Let's see why.

Now, to get an even clearer fix on worry we have to understand what I call the mathematics of worry. Here's how it works.

Two days ago Jim had a bad run-in with a customer. Because Jim hasn't learned how to prevent or cure worry, fear sets in immediately. "Will I be able to hold this customer?" As Jim evaluates this worry, his psychic apparatus breeds a second and larger worry. "What will my sales manager think of the way I goofed this deal?" This worry breeds another worry. "Will this account be reassigned to some other salesman?"

Worry has taken over Jim's entire thinking process. The "Will the account be reassigned?" breeds another worry, "Will the boss embarrass me at the next sales meeting?" This creates the biggest worry of all. "Will I lose my job?"

Now the mathematics of worry are really going to work. "How can I find another job paying as much?" "Will I have to move?" "How will my family get by when I am out of work?" "What kind of school will the kids attend?" "Will I have to start over at the bottom?" On and on it goes until one simple worry has multiplied itself into a hundred worries.

Doubts multiply. Jim begins to think he's all washed up. He

is ashamed of himself for what the other people in the company will think of him. He worries for the kids, his wife, himself.

So far we have developed two points: First, worry is essentially a mental, not a physical disease. Second, worries breed worries. But now we ask "Can anything be done about worry?" "Is there a way to cure it?" Yes, worry can be mastered but it takes deliberate action. Below are five cures. Put them to work and see how fast you can get rid of worry.

Worry Cure #1: Keep Busy

One July afternoon I was sitting on the porch of a very old but well kept resort hotel in North Carolina. I had made a speech before a group of industrialists that morning. One of the executives attending the conference was giving me his reaction to the ideas I had projected.

"I sure agree with your ideas on how to fight worry—especially the 'keep busy' approach," he commented. "You know for years I had a morale problem in my company I just couldn't pin down. The employees just didn't seem to like their jobs much. Many a morning I'd watch them enter the plant. They looked unhappy, dissatisfied, like they were entering a torture chamber. And they were even less happy when they went home. And as a result, our productivity was much too low, our accident rate was high and so was our absenteeism."

"How did you solve this?" I asked. (I knew he must have for this executive now had one of the most efficient operations in North Carolina.)

"Well," he explained, "I found the answer in a most unusual way. Four years ago I made a business trip to Japan. When I was finished I decided to go to Hong Kong and take a look at some textile operations there."

"I imagine you found them decades behind what we have here," I commented.

"Yes and no," my friend replied. "In terms of modernization

and automation they're way behind, but in terms of employee morale, which was my problem, they were far ahead.

"One morning I was being given a tour through a Hong Kong plant by a British executive," he continued. "During this plant inspection I noticed something very odd. The employees were working under terrible conditions by our standards—no air conditioning, poor lighting, excessive noise and so on. But at the same time, they appeared to be very happy and were putting forth their best efforts. They were smiling, singing, and that sort of thing.

"I noticed something else, too," he went on. "Every few minutes a worker would push himself away from his table, stand up, and run down the aisle. Then in two or three minutes he would come running back.

"I got curious about this so I asked my guide, 'Where and why do these people get up and go running?'

"'Oh,' my guide explained, 'we have a rule here when an employee needs to go to the restroom he's required to run both ways. You see we find we have a whole lot less labor difficulty if we keep everyone busy.'

"I was both amused and amazed at this. I just could imagine what would happen in my plant here in North Carolina if I tried to make people run to and from the restrooms! But gradually, the principle involved began to soak in. The busier people are, the less time they have to figure out why they don't like their work.

"Right then it hit me," my friend continued. "I saw where I had been wrong. Over the years I had gone out of my way to see how easy I could make things for my employees. I had arranged for more and more free time for them. But instead of this having a positive effect on morale, it did just the opposite.

"So, when I got back, I decided I'd use a positive approach and step up production. Understand, I didn't try to overwork my people. But I saw to it that there was no idleness.

"The result is," my friend concluded, "that my employees not only got more satisfaction from their work but they also do a better job. One rule I've learned is keep people busy and they won't get frustrated.

"Rest assured," he laughed, "I don't tell people to run to and from the restroom. But I've got them so interested in their work now that psychologically they do make the rest room trips on the double."

I've often reflected on the "Build morale by making them run to the restroom" technique. I've been able to apply the concept here in many practical situations.

Just a few months ago an executive who operates a branch sales office in Atlanta asked me to study a problem he faced. It seems he had one of those too typical offices were morale is bad with resulting high turnover and low output.

"You know," he commented, "I've got only 16 people, mostly clerical, in this operation. Yet every week I've got 4 to 6 of them coming to me for a private conference. These conferences usually are about 'I need more money,' or 'The superior in charge isn't being fair,' or 'Can I get transferred?'

"Yet," he went on, "I am about as liberal a guy as any. I pay a top wage. Holidays—hell, I give 12 paid holidays plus 2 weeks a year. Not counting the time off I give them for the doctor, personal problems and so on. I have no strict come-to-work rules. I try to be a good guy. Why don't I get results? Why do they all spend all their time complaining, feuding, and fussing?"

Well, as assigned, I studied the problem for several days. At the end of the week I made my report. "The basic problem," I explained, "is you aren't keeping your people busy enough. They simply haven't enough to do. That's why they stay so upset and produce at a relatively low level."

Immediately, I could see I had hit his psychological ouch territory. "You'd better explain," the executive snapped. "We've got a big work load here. Besides, as I explained to you when I gave you this assignment, I'm no slave driver. I'm not going to run a sweat shop."

(It took several minutes of listening to and assuring him I

did not disapprove of his conduct. As I've explained many times, you can't change anyone's thinking through argument.)

Finally, I had a chance to give some examples to support my observation. I showed him how the people didn't look forward to coming to work so most of them were late, how they didn't have enough to do to occupy their minds so they were forever conjuring mental fears, jealousy, etc. It was just 3:15 at this moment so I asked the executive what time is it. "Why, it's 3:15," he replied. "Take a look at your phone behind you," I asked. He did. "Notice anything peculiar?" "No outside lines open," he commented.

"Exactly," I said. As soon as the kids come home from school all the married women get on the phone. And they stay on the phone. They get mad at each other because someone else hangs on forever.

"Now," I continued, "I'm not saying that a phone call to the kids is not a good idea. But the excessive number and excessive length of these calls just further supports the point that your people are really bored because they don't have enough challenging work to do."

At last, my point got through.

"Well, I see what you're driving at. What can I do?"

"Actually," I replied, "you have only two alternatives. First, remove some of the people—say, cut your staff from 16 to 12. Or, second, develop more projects for these people to do."

As I suspected, the executive elected the latter course. "Why I've got dozens of jobs I want done," he said. "I've been under the impression my people had too much to do and I didn't want to overload them."

"Well, here's a case where you can have your cake and eat it too," I replied. "You can darn near double your output at no extra cost. And you'll have happier people too."

Gradually, the executive stepped up the tempo. He gave out more projects. He created a new sense of urgency about the work. He held meetings two and three times a week. He asked people to work overtime.

The result: "The people have stopped coming into my office to complain. Now they come to see me about their work—not petty problems."

Hard work *does* make happy people! And this great worry cure works in all situations, big and little. Sales executives who assign big quotas and more calls—in other words sales executives who set a fast pace—have much happier, much more productive salesmen than sales executives who let salesmen "set their own speed."

Military officers who want top morale keep their personnel *busy*. The best way to fight homesickness among troops, for example, is keep them too busy to worry.

College deans that actively encourage their faculty members to write and do research have a more contented staff than those administrators who use the "take it easy" approach. When they take it easy, they gossip, and when they gossip, discontent always results.

Parents who keep their kids busy with jobs, chores, projects, have far fewer problems than those parents who let their kids gag around.

There you have a universal principle. "Hard work makes Happy People." You can cure worry, cure depression, cure dissatisfaction just by giving people more—not less—to do.

There you have it. You won't worry if you keep busy. Try it and see. The next time you find yourself getting all frustrated, nervous, just get busy. Work is a wonderful psychic cure.

Worry Cure #2: Stop Being a Psychological Perfectionist

I'm thinking now of a professor I know on the West Coast. This individual is one of the most intelligent men I've ever known. On various intellectual tests he has come close to breaking records. His mind is exceptionally analytical. He has enormous powers of concentration. He can work 20 hours in one day and be back on the job early the next.

But where is this person today? He is an unknown Assistant Professor in an almost unknown college. Why? Not because he hasn't got the brain power, not that at all. He's getting nowhere because he hasn't been able to conquer a compulsion to be perfect. His mental process works this way. Let's assume he wants to write a paper on some phase of economics. He will try 5, 10, 20, 30 approaches to starting the paper. But he sees something wrong with each approach. He keeps looking for the perfect way. But this he cannot find, for in truth there is no perfect way. So eventually he shelves the project and starts thinking about something else. His big concern is he doesn't want to do anything wrong. Now, note this: He has worried so much about his reputation that he has no reputation.

Meanwhile his colleagues, who went through school at approximately the same time, but lacked his tremendous mental ability, have long ago surpassed him in terms of recognition, accomplishment, and income. And perhaps more important, they have achieved far more peace of mind because they are doing something instead of just thinking (worrying) about doing something.

The problem here is perfectionism.

Here's a little experiment I want you to try. For just one week keep track of the excuses you hear people give you for postponing doing something. Things like, "We can't invite friends in until we get new draperies," or "I don't have enough experience to try for a better job," or "Now isn't a good time to buy stocks—I'd better wait until conditions get back to normal," or "I'd better put this off until Monday."

Keep track, and you'll discover there are a lot of habitual postponers, people who always find a reason to put off doing something. And, if you examine the psychological processes of these people, you'll find they are, without exception, big worriers. And, unknown to them, the big cause of their worry is that they suffer from a special disease I call "psychological perfectionism." It's a bad ailment and explains why many otherwise competent people stumble through life getting nowhere and doing nothing except to mire deeper in the mud of mediocrity.

Psychological perfectionism explains why some people who aren't particularly well blessed in the brain department do much better in the standard-of-living department than their more intelligent contemporaries.

Let's assume you are an executive and assign a task to Mr. Perfectionist and the same task to Mr. Action.

Here's what you're likely to find. Mr. Perfectionist can think of 15 ways to do the project. Each of these ways has possibilities. But Mr. Perfectionist can't decide which one is best. A week later when you ask for a report he gives you a lot of gobbledegook.

Mr. Action on the other hand can only think of one way to do the job. He isn't as intelligent in an abstract way as Mr. Perfectionist, but when you ask Mr. Action for a plan, he's got one.

This is another way of saying "10 percent of something is better than 100 percent of nothing."

Believe it or not, it's better to be a compromiser than a perfectionist. A perfectionist does nothing. A compromiser makes some progress.

The perfectionist goes through life worrying about problems that can't be solved. The result is frustration, disappointment, worry, and, at best, only mediocre accomplishment.

Remember these points:

1. Don't wait for conditions to be perfect. They never will be. If you wait until you have all the information to make a decision, you'll wait forever.

2. Do something. Doing something is always better than doing nothing.

3. Be lenient with yourself. Don't try to be perfect. Try being happy instead!

Worry Cure #3: Change Your Place of Psychological Residence. Move Out of the Past into the Future

Take several minutes to read and meditate on the paragraph below. Study it until it soaks in.

A human being can live in only one of two psychological time zones. You can live in the past or you can live in the future. And the choice you make affects every facet of your personality, your life, and your happiness.

Psychologically, there can be no pure present because time is a continuously moving dimension.

I'm thinking now of a woman, about 45, single. I first met this woman, whom I'll call Eve, about 10 years ago. She had come to me as a temporary typist. Even without knowing her well I quickly discovered she was one of those past-oriented people. She spent much time telling me of her past and nothing at all about her plans for the future.

I remember one time in particular when she reached into her purse and produced a photograph of herself when she was 18 or 19. Using this picture as the take-off, she proceeded to recall her wonderful past. "I was good looking then, wasn't I?" she asked.

At that time, 10 years ago, her only apparent concern was "getting a few dollars together so I can eat." No future, no desire for a better life, no looking ahead. Just an instinctive animal urge to exist.

Well, that was 10 years ago. Just last month I chanced to meet her again. I didn't recognize her at first. An ad man for pills would say, "She's a worn-out looking 65." Eve had aged not 10 but 25 years.

I chatted with her only about 5 minutes, but in that short time period she again pulled out that picture of when she was 18! Here is a woman, wasting a life, living exclusively in the dim past.

There is an enormous difference between "Here's what I did," and "Here's what I'm going to do," or between "Here's where I've been," and "Here's where I'm going."

People can be classified in two groups—the past-oriented and the future-oriented.

How to play psychic detective. You can tell a great deal about people by the tense they use when they speak. People who are always in the past tense, "I did this," "I've done that"—people who recall the past, where they were, what they've done, etc.—are not success-oriented. They're only past tense historians.

Successful people are interested in not so much in where they have been, but where they are going. You can recognize a leader quickly by observing how much more time he spends in discussing the future than in discussing the past. Rarely does a leader discuss the past at all unless he uses it as a bridge to the future.

Let me give you an example.

Not long ago a man about 53 came to see me for help in finding a job. This fellow sat down and I asked him to tell me how I might help him. The conversation soon revealed that here was one of those big time operators, a real for sure phoney.

It was easily apparent that the individual had nothing.

Yet, in an hour's conversation, at least 55 minutes were devoted to listening to where he had been—the $300,000 he had made in a big post war army surplus deal, the multi-million dollar company he once headed, the home he once had in Palm Springs. I was treated to a rather vague, poorly pieced together history of a former "great" man.

But not once during this hour's conversation did he clearly tell me, "Now, Dr. Schwartz, here's where I want to go."

He couldn't even describe what he wanted. "I thought you might know of some situation where I'd be needed" was as close as he came to telling me what kind of job he wanted.

Now, every mental institution has at least one ex-sharecropper in real life who, in his sick imagination, owns a 100,000 acre Texas cattle ranch and a few oil wells thrown in for good measure. These are unfortunate people. But, in everyday life you'll find many—possibly most—people who, too, live in the past.

It's obviously true that employers want to know what experience a job applicant has had. But even more important, they want to know what you *want* to do and where you want to go.

Here are four practical ideas that you can use to cure worry and at the same time prepare for the good life.

1. In job interviews, be sure to bridge the gap between the

past and the future. "Where I want to go" is far more significant than "Where I've been" in helping you get the job you want.

2. In your daily affairs resist the easy temptation to discuss the past—"Here's how we used to do it." Be a *future tense* person.

3. Learn from the past but don't live there. Stop thinking about the past and you've eliminated the raw material of most worry.

4. Remember, success-oriented people in all fields live *in* and *for* the future. Identify yourself with them. The top baseball player doesn't dwell on how many home runs he hit last season. He's thinking and gunning for a better record *next* season. The real pro in the acting profession doesn't let those Oscars hold him back. He's thinking of winning another trophy next year. The former college football star doesn't replay his big game forever into later life. Instead, he begins winning in other pursuits.

Don't try living on past glory.

Here is an extra special rule to use when you decide to try for a new job. *Say good things about your previous employer.*

An executive who has hired hundreds of key people over a period of years said this to me recently. "You know, the most revealing thing about a mature person in a job interview is what does he have to say about the job he just left. The fellow who comes to me and gives me a long bitter story about how his last employer let him go—how there was a vicious underhanded coup to get him in trouble—gets no consideration at all from me.

"Now situations do develop in organizations today where an occasional fellow gets a dirty deal," he went on. "But the smart guy doesn't go around saying what a rotten deal he got. Instead he forgets this treatment and concentrates on what he can do for me."

Think about that for a minute. If you're ever let loose (that is, if you're ever involuntarily terminated), *have nothing but positive things to say about your previous employer.*

This principle of saying only good things about your past employer can be applied in other situations too.

A friend I know had planned to marry a divorcee. Everything was all set. Then the plans were called off permanently. Why? Because, in my friend's words, "She got to discussing her previous husband—what a rat he was, how unfair, what a bum and all that sort of thing. It got me scared. I figured no guy could be that bad. I figured I was headed for a similar fate if I married her. So I called it off."

The moral: Have good things to say about your past relationships—even if some of them are bitter.

I know an executive, age 43, who lost his job during a recent upheaval in his corporation. After losing his job he went around telling about how unfairly he had been treated. Oh, it was terrible. To hear him talk the whole company depended on him and yet he had been overthrown by a vicious coup.

Now, situations do develop in corporations today that are strange. That's true. But this fellow had too much negative to say. As we talked I became more convinced that he probably deserved to be let out. He was a past tense guy. Always bringing up the terrible, negative, past.

Today he is unemployable and will remain so.

I've known a lot of people in the 35-65 age range who are separated involuntarily from their jobs. How they react tells a lot. Some face the future with the "all things work together for good." And without exception in such cases, things do work out for the best. On the other side of the coin, again without exception, I've discovered that people who are severely upset about being dismissed and show this to prospective employers have a very tough time getting re-situated.

Concentrate on Foresight and Forget Hindsight

Hindsight worries go something like this. "Oh, if only I had been more careful and not had that accident. Why did I do it?" Now, it would be wonderful if we could remake the smashed car.

But we can't. Worrying about what is done won't bring back a thing.

Wives who regret, "Why was I so mean to George?" aren't helping. The past is past, dead, gone. A world full of worry won't change it one bit.

Common sense tells us that our hindsight should be 20-20. At the same time common sense should tell us that our foresight can never be 20-20.

It certainly doesn't take a genius to look back on history and see the mistakes we've made. Nor does it take a genius to look back on the stock market and see when he should have bought a certain stock and sold a certain stock. In these situations hindsight should be perfect.

But foresight can never be 20-20 and it isn't even important that it be close to 20-20.

Here's the point: It would have been far better to invest in the average common stock today than not to invest at all. This gives us an excellent example of what you can prove if you want to. Given two people, A and B, A looks at the stock market and worries. He sees danger signals. He sees things going wrong. He worries about government policies that are against the investor.

B is faced with exactly the same investment market. He feels it is better to try than not do anything. Who will have more in the long run? The answer is pretty obvious.

Don't brood over what you've done, start something else. A lot of worry stems from a reappraisal of what we have done. There is no way that we can undo what we have done. Suppose a farmer decides in the spring that he is going to plant his farm in corn. About midsummer he thinks he has made a mistake and wishes he had planted this farm in cotton. It's too late to change. The saddest words of tongue or pen are these, "it might have been." What's wrong here is to bother asking what might have been. All the talk, all the worry will never undo that which is done.

So rather than ask, "Have I done the right thing?", it is far better to accept what you've done and then go on to something else.

Worry Cure #4: Take Action

I'll bet I can describe a magazine picture you've seen a thousand times. A husband and wife are pictured in total frustration, ashtray piled high, a terrible, worried expression on their faces and a caption something like "worried over bills?"

Now, let's analyze how people meet this worry. Bills add up to more than income. So, what can we cut out?

Worry, frustration take place. "Skip the doctor bill this month and pay the dentist instead." Probably millions of husbands have told their wives, "We've got to cut down. That's all there is to it, we've got to cut down."

If as much effort were spent in devising ways to increase income as on how to cut down expenditures, these families would be out of trouble.

Here's a cure that works every time and on all kinds of worry: ACT.

Worry is a psychic disease that vanishes when action is applied.

The formula simply stated is: Don't worry. Take action instead.

Let's look at some of the psychic fears you can cure with action.

"I'm slipping on the job" worry. This worry takes on many forms. "I'm not going to move up," "The boss doesn't like me," "People see through me and think I'm a phoney."

Solution: Meet this worry two ways: First, bury yourself deeper in your work. Concentrate on doing your job better. Replace worry with positive action. Every time a doubt crosses your mind, switch mental channels fast. Keep so busy doing positive, constructive things negative doubts die from lack of mental nourishment!

"I may get sick" *worry.* This is the most intangible worry a lot of people have. It's the "evil omen" brand. "I've got an uneasy feeling," "Something's going to happen but I don't know what."

Solution: Expect the unexpected. If you knew precisely what was going to happen to you every hour of the day for 30 days, you would literally die of boredom. The fact we don't know the exact details of the future gives us excitement, fascination.

If you're worried about a friend in a far off city, call the friend and be reassured.

If you feel people laugh at your appearance, go to the beauty shop, get some new clothes, get a haircut, wear your hair differently. *But take some kind of positive action.*

If you're worried that you'll run out of money in your old age, start right now in some kind of investment program. Take positive action.

If you're afraid to get up and give talks before people, try this solution: Join the toastmasters club. Make yourself get up and speak.

Worry Cure #5: Sit Down and Count Your Blessings

Remember the old expression, "I felt sorry for myself because I had no shoes until I met a man who had no feet?"

I've learned that this is a very effective way to combat fear. You can paraphrase this in many ways. I felt sorry for myself because I made only $10,000 a year until I met a man who made only $5,000 a year. People who live in small houses shouldn't feel sorry for themselves after they meet people who live in even smaller houses.

Thank God for what you've got. Don't damn him for what you haven't got. Being grateful and calm soothes the mind.

Not long ago I was conducting a seminar for medical personnel. In the talk part of my presentation I had advanced the concept that "All things do work together for good."

This had been received with a few raised eyebrows. In the

question and answer session that followed, one fellow said to me, "Suppose you are a surgeon and must tell a patient he must have a lung removed. How can you possibly interpret this as being for the good?"

I may have been a little quick but here is how I handled it. "Tell the patient," I said, "I've got good news for you. I only have to take out one lung." They laughed, of course, but they also got the point. All things *do* work together for good.

6 RULES FOR BEATING WORRY

Worry germs will die if you'll apply these six disinfectants.

1. Keep busy. Mental idleness is the seed bed of fear, frustration, and anxiety. At the first sign of worry, get busy doing something.

2. Fight perfectionism. Stop looking for the one best way. Remember, if you wait until you're perfect, you'll be dead before you get started!

3. Take action. Action kills worry. Plunge in. Do something about the thing that worries you. Stop debating, start doing.

4. Look ahead. What's done is done. Stop trying to improve hindsight. Sharpen up your foresight instead.

5. Love the unexpected. Look forward to the unknown. Be glad life is filled with surprises. It is nature's way of preventing boredom.

6. Sit down and count your blessings. You've got more than you think!

Using Psychic Power
To Dominate
And Control
Others

5

How long has it been since someone—maybe an associate at work or a social "friend" or a neighbor—deliberately tried to insult you or embarrass you or belittle you or make you look like an ass?

Here is a bold truth. Mark it well. Remember it. Then learn how to handle it. What is this truth? Just this: *There are some people who want to see you slip, see you suffer misfortune, see you get into a real tight spot, see you lose money, miss out on promotions.*

These are the people—these knockers—who can hardly wait to say, "He got just what he deserved," or "He always thought he was so much, now look at him." These people, and there are many of them, take a wicked form of delight in seeing things go wrong for you.

Knockers work on a personal level. They specialize in making negative reflections on your character, your intelligence, your opinions and ideas, your possessions, and your friends.

Learning how to handle belittlers, critics, and related forms of petty people is an absolute essential in your success-building program. People who delight in driving you down require special handling. The pages that come next show how. Study these suggestions. Once you've mastered the technique of handling petty people, you'll tap a new source of inner strength and peace of mind. And you'll protect yourself from a trap that has cost other success-minded people fortunes.

You Win When You Refuse to Fight

In the early 1960's a very capable former high school principal was running for Congress in a midwestern state. This fellow had an excellent record. His integrity was tops. He was intelligent and he looked like a sure winner.

But about midway in the campaign a small rumor got started to the effect that at a teacher's convention in the capital city three or four years ago he had had an affair with a single teacher. When the candidate got wind of this tale, he was furious. It was a lie and he proceeded to prove it.

At every political rally he made a point to denounce this vicious lie. Now, the rumor had never gained force. Most of the voters hadn't even heard it until the candidate himself raised it. But as always happens in situations like this, the more the educator professed innocence the more the people believed he was guilty. They asked the obvious question: "If he's innocent, why does he make such a point of pleading not guilty?"

It was like pouring a truck load of gasoline on a bonfire. The candidate, while truly innocent, convinced so many voters that he was guilty that he was soundly defeated. And worst and saddest of all, his own wife eventually came to believe it, too. While she did not divorce him, their intimate relationship was forever destroyed.

Many, many fine capable people have crippled their careers by stooping to answer wild charges that few people believe. But when we rush in to deny an accusation, people, at least many of them, automatically believe the charges are true. Why else would you make such a point of defending yourself?

Very early in my career as a college professor I encountered an experience that taught me much about how to handle snipers. I had been made Chairman of an Exclusions Committee. This Committee was set up to develop some policy recommendations on what to do with students who had been expelled from college because of low grades.

After numerous meetings the committee was finally ready to report to the full faculty. I gave the report and sat down. Immediately Professor "Sniper" (Sniper wasn't his real name, of course, but it sure fits) got up and proceeded to blast away at every aspect of the report. He called the report "weak," "stupid," "as immature as its principal author (me)." His remarks were mean, low, vicious, and calculated.

As he talked I felt myself getting angry. I, and the others on the committee, had worked hard. I wanted to fight back. I wanted to jump up and retaliate. But somehow, I forced myself to remain outwardly calm.

After his tirade, which lasted twice as long as my oral report, the Chairman of the meeting said, "Professor Schwartz, do you care to comment on Professor 'Sniper's' remarks?" I arose and replied, "I'm sincerely sorry the report displeases Professor ———, but speaking for the committee, it represents the best of our combined thinking. Speaking for myself, I'm ready for a vote to accept or reject it."

There were a few other comments and then the vote. Four to one in favor of the report!

Afterwards, one of the senior professors, a grey-haired fellow with almost 40 years' experience on college faculties, drew me aside. I'll always remember what he said to me. "Schwartz, I'm glad you didn't stoop to fighting just now. You had every right to get mad as hell and answer those charges in the same manner he made them. Just about everybody in this room today thought his remarks were out of order. But had you called him names, you would have lost support. The people here would have thought you were as small as he. Answering him the way you did made you appear bigger. It actually added stature to the report.

"Let me pass on to you a little of my experience for what it's worth," he went on. "We call ourselves civilized but there are varying degrees of being civilized. When the under-civilized fellow hears a comment he doesn't like, he's quick to use his fists and literally try to beat the other fellow. The grade above him, the average-civilized person, doesn't use his fists, he uses his tongue. He fights back with cruel, vicious belittling words.

"Now, the super-civilized person doesn't use either hands or tongue. He simply refuses to fight back! He knows that the only way to win when someone attacks you on a personal basis is just to ignore him."

Laugh Away the Criticism

All the really top politicians learn that the only smart thing to do is to refuse to fight the obvious lies. In every presidential campaign I can remember there is always the rumor that one candidate's wife is an alcoholic or is maritally unhappy with the candidate.

Franklin Delano Roosevelt made friends and he made enemies. He was controversial. But he consistently made more friends than enemies. This made him a winner.

Almost from his first day as President, critics were taking pot shots at Roosevelt. Over the years these attacks grew worse. They reached a climax in 1940 when Roosevelt decided to break with an old tradition and run for a third term. Many people were really mad at Roosevelt by then. And much of this anger was released at Roosevelt on a *personal* basis—attacks on Eleanor, digs at the Roosevelt sons for receiving military commissions the short-cut way, digs at the apparent special and unusual privileges which were passed out to friends of the family.

The attacks were calculated to make Roosevelt mad, to get him upset, to cause him to lose his balance, to make him slug it out in a dirty, negative way.

But how did FDR react? Did he defend his actions? Did he try to deny the special privileges his family enjoyed? Did he accept the challenge to fight in the gutter? No, not Roosevelt!

Instead the master politician, the political pro, handled the people who were trying to drive him down in a classic manner. This is how he did it. In a speech which was on the national networks, Roosevelt had this to say:

> Eleanor [his wife] doesn't care what they say about her. My sons don't mind what they say about them. And I sure don't care what the critics say about me. But folks, Fala [his dog], Fala is getting mad!

Roosevelt simply laughed the criticisms out of the campaign.

Next time you're tempted to fight back, set the record straight and answer the lies other people say about you, remember FDR. Roosevelt won because he resisted the temptation to fight petty people. You will too!

Go Out and Make Your Enemy Your Friend

Here's a third way to deal with people who are deliberately trying to knock you down.

I had a most unusual and really heartwarming chat with a salesman in Charlotte recently. It was unusual because what my friend did set him apart from the vast crowd of so-called salesmen. And it was heart-warming because this fellow had won a personal victory doing the unnatural thing. Let me tell you about it.

It seems my friend, Carl S., who sold bricks, was being given a really tough time by a competitor's salesman. The competing salesman regularly went around the territory telling architects and contractors that Carl's company was unreliable, his bricks were no good, and that business was so bad Carl's company would soon fold.

Carl explained to me that he didn't feel the success of his competitor actually hurt him too much in the pocketbook. But it was a nuisance and did make him boil inside. (Carl was really vocal on this.) "I was so damn mad at him on more than one occasion that I confess I wanted to break a stack of bricks over his fat head.

"Well," Carl explained, "one Sunday morning in church the minister preached a sermon on the subject, 'Bless Those Who Despitefully Use You.'

"I drank in every word," Carl continued. "Just the Friday before my competitor had cost me an order for 250,000 bricks by convincing a contractor that our white bricks would turn a greenish color after they were put up. This was a complete lie and if ever I felt like I was being despitefully used, it was now."

Carl went on. "The minister offered this advice. 'Go out and make your enemy your friend.' The minister was very demanding on this. He contended—and he had a whole lot of examples to back him up—that you can turn an enemy into a friend simply by going out of your way to do a good turn for the enemy.

"That afternoon as I was arranging my next week's schedule, which is a Sunday afternoon habit of mine, I noticed where one of my customers in Virginia was requesting bids for bricks for a new office building. Now, the bricks specified were not the type my company could manufacture. But they were identical to the best line my competitor sold. I also knew that that foul-mouthed competitor had never been able to get to first base with this contractor.

"Here is where I faced a tough decision. If I followed my minister's advice I would get in touch with my competitor, tell him about this opportunity, and wish him luck. But, if I did what I really wanted to do, I'd simply feel: it'll serve the b———— right if he never hears about this."

"What did you do?" I asked.

"Well, I struggled for a while. But the minister's voice, 'Go out and make your enemy your friend,' kept overpowering me. Finally, perhaps because I just wanted to prove the minister was wrong, I picked up the phone and dialed my competitor's home. His wife answered and I asked to speak with him."

"Was he surprised?" I asked half laughing.

"Was he!" Carl exclaimed. "You can imagine his immediate reaction. He was almost too embarrassed to speak. I told him—quite politely, I might add—about the Virginia deal."

"He stammered around a little but it was pretty obvious he did appreciate the help. In fact, as I talked to him I decided to go even one more step. I promised I'd call the contractor in Virginia and recommend him for the order."

"What happened after that?" I asked, for I was eager to learn how the competitor acted when the fellow he had been belittling had done him such a good turn.

"Well," Carl explained, "the good turn on my part produced some amazing results. Not only did my competitor stop telling lies about me but—get this—he's even sent some business he couldn't handle my way. Now, besides clearing the air, I've even made money following my minister's advice, 'Go out and make your enemy your friend.'

"And there's one other result, Dr. Schwartz."

"What's that?" I asked.

"I just feel better," Carl replied.

Go out and make your enemy your friend—that's the third way to battle the petty fellow who's working overtime to make you look bad.

Learn the Victory Sentence

I had a warm and interesting chat several months ago with a remarkable woman who has been a teacher in the Cleveland Public Schools for 32 years. We were discussing the continued problem all teachers have: the problem of how to help the two or three students in every class who are laughed at or bullied or otherwise persecuted by another group of students.

"It's always hurt me," she began, "to see children who are just a little different from the rest picked on by the classroom bullies.

"Often these persecuted children," she continued, "are

brighter, more sensitive, and more perceptive than the rest. In my early years as a teacher I was at a loss as to how to cope with this. I tried sympathy but that really was no cure. But finally I found a solution that works."

"What's that?" I asked, for I had seen this very same problem many times in education even on the university level.

"Simply this," she replied. "When I see a youngster who has done nothing wrong being tormented by other children, I take the individual aside and ask him to write what I call the 'Victory Sentence' 100 times."

"Tell me, what is the Victory Sentence?"

"Oh, it's nothing too profound I guess," she smiled, "but it does work amazing results. The Victory Sentence is this: *I will ignore pettiness in other people.* Later, I discuss the full meaning with the child who has been offended. I show him how terribly wrong it is to be upset by the taunting of others."

I remarked to this fine lady how unusual her method was, unusual in that the bullies were not punished while the innocent child wrote a sentence 100 times.

"Oh, I've been criticized for my method," she replied. "Some teachers feel I should punish the bullies and try to solve things that way. But I can prove my method is right.

"All through life from the school playground to the Executive Suite there are those who torment others," she continued. "I'm not so sure we can cure the tormentors. So I concentrate on helping the tormented develop a resistance to petty attacks.

"Let me show you something," she went on. (Here she opened her desk, removed a neat-appearing file and produced a letter.) "Read this."

It was a letter from a United States Senator expressing his personal thanks 27 years later for having learned the Victory Sentence, "*I will ignore the pettiness in other people.*"

Don't you wish a teacher had taught you the Victory Sentence back there in the fifth grade? I know I do.

Next time you're under petty attack, remember the Victory Sentence: *I will ignore pettiness in other people.*

Be Glad You're Criticized. It's Proof
You're Growing!

The most sniped at, criticized, and bitterly attacked person in the United States today is not a criminal. He is not a murderer or rapist awaiting the death sentence in some jail. He is not a spy, and he is not even a communist.

He is the President of the United States.

And the person most criticized 5, 10, 15, 30 years ago was also the President of the United States. The man with the biggest job is also the man most attacked. That's true in every walk of life. Big job means big criticism.

Have you ever paused to notice who isn't sniped at? Check and you'll discover the only people free of the belittling tactics of petty people are those who are at the bottom of life's totem pole. In a corporation, the division chief may be criticized regularly by jealous subordinates and associates. But who knows the janitor?

In Hollywood, top actors are belittled regularly; the starlets escape.

Generals are regularly torn to pieces. Privates escape.

The bigger you grow, the more you can expect to be criticized.

So don't think it is abnormal when people try to beat you down. Regard it as a sign that you're growing.

The president of a relatively young but fast growing manufacturing company gave me his views on criticism. "I learned soon after I started this company," he began, "that how I react to criticism has made the difference between being a success in this business or failing. And it's such a simple 'secret,' most people won't put it to use."

"What is it?" I asked.

"Just this. Concentrate 100 percent of the time on trying to do what is right and forget about criticism. If you do your job the best you can and don't let the critics push you off course, you'll come out on top. Let me give you an example.

"About ten years ago I had some careful engineering studies made that showed it was economically sound to invest up to $20,000 in machinery to replace one worker.

"So, I started doing that. I bought a packaging machine that cost $57,000 that replaced four workers. But did I come under fire! In a small town like this everybody soon knows all the news. The local paper ran a series of editorials about what I had done. People accused me of 'worshipping machinery' and 'not thinking of workers' and all that sort of thing.

"All this unfavorable comment almost convinced me I was wrong. Certainly I didn't like having most of the people around here thinking I was an S.O.B. *But I just couldn't compromise with what I felt was right.* I stuck with the policy and it has paid off. Despite the fact that I've put in almost half a million worth of new machinery, I continually find I need more people too for the many jobs machines can't do. Since I started my machine replacement policy a decade ago, I've more than doubled my work force.

"But had I failed to do what was right the odds are this business wouldn't even exist today, let alone be so successful."

There you have Rule 2 for handling people who want to drive you down: Expect to be sniped at. It's proof you're getting bigger. And never compromise with what you know is right.

Here's an excerpt of a letter from a friend who is an author. Read it.

"I'm not at all disappointed about the review in ————. I feel really complimented that out of about 200 books published that week they chose mine for review. I've written four others and that magazine never bothered with them. That they didn't like the book isn't nearly as important to me as is the fact that they thought it was important enough to review. It makes me feel like I'm coming up in the literary world."

Many successful old-timers in entertainment and political fields say, "It's not too important what the critics say so long as they spell your name right."

The bigger you grow, the more apt you are to be criticized.

Criticism is proof you're growing. So, if you must worry, worry because you aren't criticized enough.

Chances are you're thinking at this point that I'm a little theoretical about how to handle mean, vicious people who delight in trying to hurt you.

But I'm not. Read this.

Recently, a fine, intelligent, and competent woman about 60 came to see me about a job problem. A few months before I had helped this lady find a job in advertising after the untimely death of her under-insured executive husband. This was her first paid job in 35 years and she regarded me as a sort of employment godfather.

"Dr. Schwartz, I'm so troubled I don't know what to do," she began. "I'm afraid I'm going to lose my job." At this point, showing signs of severe and prolonged emotional distress, she began to cry.

I finally soothed her and asked her to explain.

"You see," she went on, "I work directly with two other women, both considerably younger than I. To put it bluntly, Dr. Schwartz, they're out to get me! We all three have the same boss but these two women are doing everything they can to make me and my work look bad."

Being specific, my friend went on to explain that she was belittled repeatedly in front of others, was ignored at lunch, was the chief object for ridicule in the ladies lounge, a victim of the classic tear-the-other-person-to-pieces routine.

Finally, about cried out, she said, "What can I do?"

I thought a few moments, then replied, "Mrs. ———, in your own mind, thinking very objectively, do you honestly believe you're doing a good job?"

To this she responded with a very positive, "Yes, I do. The job is no problem."

Then I asked her this question: "Do you think your boss is stupid?"

This question both bewildered and amused her just a bit.

But half smiling she admitted that he seemed to be an intelligent and apparently fair man.

"Then," I replied, "you have nothing to be concerned about. Just continue to do your very best job."

"But suppose I get fired?" she again raised that troubling question.

"Look at it this way," I answered. "If you do your very best work and these petty people convince the boss you should go, then you would be a fool to work for him."

I succeeded in helping my friend realize that an executive who can't separate troublemakers from those who are sincerely trying to do good work really isn't an executive. As it turned out, the boss proved to be a very perceptive fellow (most executives are!). And the two troublemakers were soon dealt with, and rather severely, too.

What's the moral? Just this: When other people on your job go gunning for you with various negative, embarrassing, petty attacks just (a) concentrate on doing your job (b) remain polite and friendly and (c) ignore their petty attacks.

Do these three things and you win every time!

Remember also, even though he may not show it in obvious ways, in 9 cases out of 10, the boss knows who's on the ball and who isn't.

When You're Wrong, Admit It

When Ted Kennedy was running for the U. S. Senate, it didn't take much research by his opposition to discover the now famous "Harvard Episode." The details aren't important here but Mr. Kennedy, as a student, had been expelled from Harvard for cheating.

Potentially, this was a political hydrogen bomb! Think for a moment of the political harvest the opposition could reap with evidence which cast serious doubts on the basic honesty, integrity, and morality of Mr. Kennedy.

The normal, typical reaction would have been to try and lie

out of it, to develop some kind of "explanation" which would prove this wasn't really true. How Senator Kennedy dealt with this situation proved he knows how to handle people who want to drive him down.

What did he do when asked about this experience?

He admitted it freely. Senator Kennedy expressed what appeared to be sincere regret, admitted he had made a bad mistake, and said in effect, "I'm sorry for what I did. It was wrong. I have no defense."

Now, analyze his reaction very carefully. You can learn a basic success principle. How can you fight a man who admits he's made a mistake?

What can the opposition say? The answer: *nothing*.

Instead of being hurt by his Harvard experience, Senator Kennedy turned it into advantage. Here's why. First, when he admitted he had cheated in school, he *humanized* himself. He identified himself with the average man. (After all, who has not cheated in school at one time or another?) Second, admitting his guilt won sympathy for Senator Kennedy. Who hasn't heard the basic truth many times: "Let him who has never sinned cast the first stone." And, of course, a lot of people feel, "There, but for the grace of God, go I."

Finally, only *honest* people *admit* their mistakes. So Mr. Kennedy had to be honest for he admitted his error.

There's a big lesson here. When you're wrong, admit it. And you can come out of it smelling like a rose. But if you are guilty and you try to lie out of it, you're in serious trouble.

Maybe you're wondering why some people go out of their way to attack you, make you look bad, humiliate you, get even with you and in other ways try to undercut you. Basically, here's the answer. Such people are intensely dissatisfied with themselves. They are unhappy. Often they have a bad marital relationship. These folks hate themselves. Usually, this person hates his job. He is jealous, often almost insanely so. But not being intellectually or morally honest, this person takes his hate out on you. He is too immature to recognize his real problems.

Even though you and I may not have met, I feel I know something about you. For one thing, I know you aren't a cynical knocker. You are not trying to get ahead by knocking other people down. You see, knockers never bother to read books such as this. They already have all the answers.

Remember, the purpose of this chapter is to help you understand how to handle people who want to drive you down. The purpose is *not* to show you how to convert these petty people, much as I share with you a wholesome desire to see this done.

Look at it this way. "Knocking" in all of its many forms, belittling other people "organizational sabotage," malicious gossip, petty attacks, is a form of psychological virus. What I've outlined here will vaccinate you against it. But the principles set forth won't cure the person who has this disease.

You have made a giant step toward personal peace, happiness, and when you recognize this basic truth: *The majority of people fit in the petty classification. Only a small minority of us qualify as big thinkers.*

And this is very important: *When you accept the petty person's invitation to fight, you lose.*

TEST YOUR REACTIONS TO PETTY PEOPLE

Situation	Typical But Wrong Way to Handle It	Right Way—How Big People Handle It
1. A neighbor spreads gossip to another neighbor about you, your teenage children, your finances, etc.	Retaliate. Fight back. Counterattack with gossip about the neighbor who started the gossip.	Ignore it. Remember that gossip is the delight of the petty masses.
2. Fellow employee makes you look incompetent or stupid in a memo to your boss.	Write a memo to the boss attacking the person who wrote the memo about you.	Take it as a compliment. You are now important enough to be attacked.

3. You are threatened by "blackmail." "If you do such and such, I'll do such and such to hurt you."	Back down. Pay the blackmailer. Run.	Do what is right. Act fearlessly.
4. A competitor spreads rumors about you, your product, your company.	Counteract with negative information about the competitor.	Sincerely try to make the enemy a friend. Do not retaliate.
5. You are assassinated on a personal basis.	Worry, grow frustrated, plan a counterattack.	Laugh at it. Often these attacks can be very entertaining

TECHNIQUES FOR PETTINESS PROTECTION

In capsule form, here's how to protect yourself from the pettiness in other people.

1. Remember, you win when you refuse to fight petty people.

2. Learn to laugh at criticism.

3. Go out and make your enemy your friend. Do a favor for him and see what happens!

4. Learn the victory sentence: "I will ignore pettiness in other people." It's part of the thinking apparatus of all top people.

5. Be glad you're criticized. It's the best proof you can have that you're growing in influence.

6. When you're wrong, admit it. Don't try to lie out of a situation if you are guilty. When you admit you're wrong, you look big, honest, and human to others.

How To Gain Courage
And Overcome Fears
That Are Holding
You Back

6

Now we come to a very critical phase in your success-building program. Let me set the stage by recalling two famous American battles of the last century, The Battle of the Alamo and Custer's Last Stand. The details of these battles are known to every child. We've all read about them and seen them reenacted in movies and TV plays. In both cases a comparative handful of Americans were wiped out fighting against tremendous odds.

As these battles are romantically described, the implication is that only superhuman, superbrave, and supereffective Americans were involved. I've heard someone say, not once but many times, "We just don't have heroes like that anymore."

I greatly enjoy American history and often discuss it with historians. About a year ago, when we were discussing these two famous incidents, an historian gave me his view. "You know," he said, "we always portray these soldiers as terrific heroes. But do you want to know what I feel made them fight so hard and so effectively?"

I assured my friend I was interested in his opinion.

"Because," he continued, "they could not surrender and they could not escape. There was only one thing for them to do. Fight until they were dead.

"When soldiers can't surrender and can't retreat, they fight like hell," he added.

My friend and I talked on. We reviewed some of the "no surrender, no retreat" tactics military leaders have used since the first days of organized warfare.

In World War II perhaps the most striking example was the suicide attacks on U. S. ships by Japanese kamikazi pilots. These were prearranged suicide ventures. Japanese airmen would take off from their bases knowing two things: (a) they could not surrender and (b) they could not return to base. Result: they did tremendous damage to our naval forces.

Now, what does this have to do with personal success? Just this: great military or physical victories are won when physical retreat is impossible. And great psychological victories are won when psychological retreat is impossible.

Here is the law: *Chances for success are maximized when every possible psychological escape hatch is closed.* Repeat. Chances for success in any project are increased when we deliberately cut off our avenues of psychological escape.

Now, let's develop this law and let's learn it!

Be Big: Say, "I Am Responsible," and Watch Yourself Move Up

About a year ago I was visiting in the home of a Memphis business executive. We were talking about psychological escape hatches. Then he said to me, "I've got a tape I want you to hear. I need your advice."

Here I got a big surprise. I expected to hear a tape of a business discussion. Instead, it turned out to be a recording of a conversation between my friend, who happened to be a church deacon, two other deacons, and the minister of the church. The recording, I learned, had been made in the very room in which we were sitting, the library of my friend's home. The occasion was a discussion between the deacons and the ministers regarding two big related problems the church was facing: dealing with attendance and troubles with the budget.

(My friend, whose hobby is electronics, explained to me he frequently records key discussions of this kind so he can later review precisely what was said and the way it was said. In this case, the other two deacons and the minister were unaware the conversation was being recorded.)

We sat there and listened for almost an hour. Then my friend looked at me and asked, "Well, what do you think? We've had this fellow as our minister for two years. Since then average attendance is off 22 percent and church collections are down 19 percent. Should we continue with him or should we request a replacement?"

(It was admittedly a rather cold way to evaluate something of this delicate nature but someone must make such decisions.)

"Well," I suggested, "let's analyze the minister's explanation as to why the congregation seems to be disintegrating."

"You heard the tape," my friend began. "What did he say? First, he blamed the trend of the times—everything from too many sporting events on Sunday, to people are too busy, to the general decline in national morality.

"Second," my friend continued, "he blamed the lay leadership. We aren't supporting him on his various projects. We aren't following through. We're bogged down. We're not giving enough time to the church."

"It seems to me," I injected, "like he's put the blame everywhere except where it belongs—on himself."

I then explained to my friend that when trouble develops we can place the blame in three places. We can blame

1. Fate
2. Other people
3. Ourselves

Then we reviewed the minister's explanation. It was quite clear he blamed fate ('the decline in morality,' 'trend of the times,' and so on.) And it was also clear he blamed other people ('the lay leadership is not behind me,' etc.)

"Well, what would you do?" my friend, who has a way of wanting to get directly to the point, asked.

"If you are firmly convinced that this fellow does not and cannot see that he must assume full responsibility for this problem, then," I said, "your course of action is obvious. It isn't pleasant but it's the only right thing to do."

Let me illustrate this another way. I am writing this book. Correct? You are reading this book. Right?

Now if you don't understand what I'm writing about, it isn't because you are stupid. No sir, friend. Rather, it's because I did not explain it clearly. As you read this book, the burden of explanation is 100 percent on me. It's not your responsibility to get smarter. It's my responsibility to write clearer.

In the classroom, if the student doesn't learn, the teacher hasn't taught. Now this looks like a hard philosophy. It is. But it's the only way we move ahead. The teacher who blames fate ('backward students') or other people ('parents who won't cooperate') may be able to rock along for a lifetime as a "satisfactory" teacher. But that individual will never be great and will never rise to the summit in educational circles.

The physician who chalks up a failure to fate ('it was just one of those unexplainable things') or blames other people ('the patient just didn't cooperate') can probably get by O. K. But that physician will never be great.

Only when we accept personal responsibility for failure do we begin to see ways for improvement.

In sales development programs I frequently tell trainees, "If the customer doesn't buy, the salesman hasn't sold." I guess I've made a lot of salesmen angry with this comment. But I've also helped make a lot of them successful. A salesman can figure out plausible explanations by the dozen to explain a turndown. But it's only when a salesman accepts the responsibility for defeat that he grows big enough to see solutions to future victories.

Once when I was sitting behind the dugout at a baseball game, a player who had just flied out to right field came back to the bench and said to the manager, "The wind is too strong." The manager retorted very fast, "Wind, hell. You just didn't hit the damn ball hard enough."

How's that for a success philosophy? Sure, the coach could have said, "You're right, sonny. It was that mean old wind." Instead, the coach said the truth. "You just didn't hit the damn ball hard enough."

Shortly after President Kennedy took office, the now famous Bay of Pigs Invasion was staged. It was a miserable flop. Possibly it was one of the most poorly executed maneuvers in our history. No one knew what he was doing. There was no coordination of effort. The net effect was defeat.

Now, Kennedy was President. But he had been in office only a few weeks. Much of the thinking and intelligence to support this strike was inherited from the previous administration.

President Kennedy could have passed at least some of the buck to the preceding administration. And doubtlessly his weaker political advisors probably told him to do this.

But what did Kennedy do? He did the unusual. He accepted full responsibility for the failure. He did not go political (which is synonymous with going weak) on this matter. He told the American people in effect "Whatever flop took place, my administration did it."

And by assuming responsibility he did two things: One, he proved his size and won respect from his political enemies. Two, by taking the blame, *by plugging up his escape hatch*, he virtually nullified the Cuban Invasion as a political issue. Remember, when a person says, "I'm guilty," "Blame me," "It's my fault," he demonstrates he is a big man. And people respect big men.

Develop the Feeling of Responsibility

One bit of wisdom that has paid off for me a thousand-fold is this: if the trainee hasn't learned, the trainer hasn't taught.

For example, I have found this concept very useful in making talks. I've heard many speakers in pretalk briefings say something to their host like, "I sure hope you have a warm audience tonight," or "I hope they're wide awake."

Now, I never have these worries. And for one simple reason: I never place any responsibility on the audience for being a good audience. If they get bored, it's my fault. If they don't laugh, it's not their fault, it's mine. *The burden of proof is on me*, not on them. And this forces me to put forth the maximum 100 percent effort every time.

I had a long talk with a salesman recently. He went on and on about what a rotten deal he got. He was doing terribly. He was not meeting his quota and he felt he was in the company doghouse.

"Well," I asked, "what do you feel is responsible for this?"

"A number of things. Make no mistake about it—it's not my fault. I've got the worst territory. The people I've got as accounts are the worst. But that's not all of it. I've got more competition. I've told my sales manager it's plain unfair. But he's prejudiced and just doesn't understand my situation."

He went on and on. In his 20-minute explanation of what's behind his failure, not once did he mention that he was responsible, that he didn't know the product or he didn't have technique or he was off base in some way.

Escape Hatching in Marriage

I'm sure most adult men have seen the card I'm thinking of on the excuses a wife can give for not having intercourse with her husband. It's not a very nice card and is frankly embarrassing to men with character. Nevertheless, the reasons given—which number around 35 or 40—is creative in the sense that every excuse imaginable has been devised. Yet all of them sound perfectly plausible. Everything from the "I've got a headache" to "I'm too tired" to "Go to sleep, dear, you've got to get up early tomorrow" to, of course, "escape hatches" that aren't the type to print here, but which you as a mature adult understand.

Now, marital problems can stem from many causes. But the fact is obvious that unsatisfactory sexual relationships is a big one—probably the biggest. Don't you wonder how many marriages would be more successful if "escape hatching" weren't so prevalent in this intimate area of human relations? Wives who find all sorts of excuses to ration marital love generally end up unloved, unadmired, unwelcome, and unmarried.

How Many Escape Hatches Are Possible?

There is, literally, no limit to the number and variety of escape hatches. This is true because the person addicted to escape hatching can invent any number of escape hatches to protect himself in any situation.

A young man I know recently was graduated from college with—get this—340 quarter hours credit! This was almost double the number needed for a degree. Why? Simply this: He was afraid of going out in the competitive world. He reasoned, "I feel safe in school. If the right kind of opportunity doesn't come along, I'll stay put," and he "stayed put" because the "right opportunity" never seems to "find" such people. Now, guess what he did when he finally graduated? You're right. He enrolled in law school.

He'll be safe there for another three to five years. After that, he'll develop some other device to avoid meeting the real world.

WHAT'S YOUR ESCAPE HATCH?

Situation	Escape Hatch	Real Problem
1. Traveling salesman develops habit of coming home Thursday nights even though he's expected Friday.	"My wife needs me. She's overloaded with work. I'd better be home."	Saleman doesn't like his job. Wife need gives him his way out.
2. Executive goes back on promise to raise employee's pay.	"We've developed a real budget problem. Just as soon as we get back in shape we'll take care of you."	Executive is afraid his superior will think life is getting too liberal. Wants to look good.
3. Father is under family pressure to go to the State Fair.	"We can't afford it," or "I've got to work."	He wants to enjoy *his* recreation and not provide his family with what they want.
4. "Friend" cancels invitation to attend your party.	"Have a terrible headache," or "Can't get a sitter," or "We're expecting out of town guests."	Doesn't want to go.

Here's the positive philosophy. It's not easy. But it works.

If your company isn't buying you to the point of giving you a raise, don't blame the company, blame you.

If your marriage partner isn't loving you to the degree you want to be loved, don't blame the partner, blame you.

The burden of proof is on you, not on the world!

If your customers aren't buying, don't blame them, blame you.

"If you're a preacher and the congregation falls asleep on Sunday morning, what is wrong?" I've asked many people to report on this. They'll say: "Room is too warm," or "They were out late the night before." Only rarely does one hear the truth. "The minister bored them to sleep."

How We Grow Dependent on Psychological Escape Hatches

How do we grow dependent upon psychological escape hatching? There are just two ways. First is never being taught strong self-reliance by those in a position to exercise strong direction over you such as your parents. Second is never teaching yourself to stand on your own two psychological feet.

A widowed mother, now about 60, and her divorced son, now about 35, provide such an example. It is an extreme case. But bear in mind less developed situations are exceedingly common.

The mother is a strong, highly self-reliant individual who never found real satisfaction in her marriage. Her husband died when the son was 20. The son, Jimmy, in mother's eyes was always very bright and very right. But when teachers gave him a low mark mother would say, "There, there, Jimmy, don't worry. You know it wasn't your fault. I'll speak with your teacher."

This was the typical pattern. In traffic court, the judge was mean and unfair. In athletic tryouts, the coaches were prejudiced; in school plays the teachers couldn't recognize talent. Jimmy learned two things: (a) other people were always treating him unfairly and (b) mother would always take his part.

When Jimmy got married, his mother gave him the send off you'd expect. "Now Jimmy, if things don't work out, remember your mother always loves you and will help you in any way possible."

Naturally, the marriage quickly developed rough spots (what marriage doesn't) and mother was right there telling Jimmy, "You know Janice is wrong for you. It's awful the way she misunderstands you. She just doesn't know how to treat you like I do." It was made clear to Jimmy that he wasn't responsible for the state of affairs. This went on. The divorce came. Back to mother came Jimmy. About the same time he lost his job in the ad business because "the agency head wasn't smart enough to see Jimmy was a creative genius."

Eventually, Jimmy was placed in a private mental hospital. He had to be released soon "because the hospital didn't understand him." This went on. More hospitals, same story. More jobs were gotten through friends only to be quickly lost because "they aren't fair to Jimmy" or "they are jealous of Jimmy so they let him go."

Things are really pathetic now. The money left by Jimmy's father is gone. Mother has a low-pay job that provides barely enough for the two of them to exist. All this tragedy because mother did not close the escape hatches and teach Jimmy self-reliance.

This is a rather extreme case but it does illustrate how some people fail to learn the two basic laws of (a) responsibility, and (b) close the psychological escape hatches.

As I reflect on this troublesome case, I find myself comparing Jimmy's mother with our Mother Cat. We have a fine productive cat who has kittens two or three times a year. But Mother Cat instinctively knows to let the baby kittens shift for themselves at the right time. Mommy Cat feeds them and protects them and loves them as long as necessary. But when the time comes, baby cats must find their own food.

Isn't it a shame so many people lose nature's instinct and hold their young back instead of pushing them out of the nest?

Now, much dependence on psychological escape hatches and failure to be responsible goes directly to parental influence. True, young people who are victims of this type of influence aren't able to do much about it while they are children.

But once they are aware of what is happening, they do have a chance assuming they use the full strength of the law of "total commitment."

I'm thinking now of another young man, son of a college official. When the boy was young, his parents divorced. The boy stayed with his mother who was a dominant person and made all the decisions for the boy. He, too, reached the age of 20 a helpless, cowardly, inferior, whipped person. But a long, grueling, applied effort whereby he was psychologically weaned and made to stand on his own mental feet cured him to the degree he is now making fine progress in the world.

We know this: People who follow the two basic commandments—close the escape hatches and act 100 percent responsible —do win the big jobs, the money, the beautiful women, and all that is good.

"I can always return to mother," "I can always go back to my old job," "I can avoid contact with the world," these are stepping stones to mental disaster.

More times than I can remember, after a lecture or speech or seminar, someone has asked me in a voice that indicated more amazement than disbelief or distrust, "Dr. Schwartz, do you honestly believe we should accept full responsibility for what happens to us? Are you really saying if things don't go my way, it's my fault?"

I'm not sure these people are fully satisfied when I say, "YES. I do. There are no ifs, ands, or buts about it. To achieve the most possible in the way of peace of mind, you must adopt the captain of your own fate attitude."

I've simply racked up too much evidence to feel otherwise. I assure them that we're not talking about one man's personal opinion. We're talking about a universal law of success. You can no more argue with this law than argue with the law of gravity.

100 PERCENT COMMITTED PSYCHE CAN'T BE STOPPED

There were many miracle victories in World War II. But one that stands out in the sinking of the German battleship, the Bismarck. The giant German battlewagon was a tremendous vessel and a terrifying threat to Allied shipping. British Intelligence learned that the Bismarck was leaving the North Sea area and was headed for the open sea where it was certain to have many field days sinking British and American ships.

When Churchill learned of this he made a decision: the Bismarck had to be sunk. His staff officers advised him this couldn't be done. The logic of the moment showed the British obviously lacked ships, aircraft, and fire power to do the job.

But all the negative talk didn't discourage Churchill. He was determined.

C. S. Forester, in his excellent article describing this famous sea battle of World War II, gives this authentic account of Winston Churchill's conversation with the fleet flag officer.

"From out of the box came the unmistakable tones of the Prime Minister's voice. 'Your job is to sink the Bismarck,' said the boss. 'That is your overriding duty. No other considerations are to have any weight whatever."

"Yes, Mr. Prime Minister."

"What about Ramillies? What about Rodney?"

"Orders are being issued at this moment, Mr. Prime Minister."

"Revenge, Force?"

"They have their orders."

"You're taking every possible step to see that Bismarck is going to be sunk?"

"Yes, Mr. Prime Minister."

"Not only the possible steps, not only the easy steps and the obvious steps, but the difficult steps and the almost impossible steps, and all the quite impossible steps you can manage as well. The eyes of the whole world are upon us."

"You don't have to remind me about that, Mr. Prime Minister."

"Well, remember. Sink the Bismarck. Good-bye." [1]

In short order, the Bismarck was sunk. It was quite a battle but the Bismarck was sunk.

Now suppose, just suppose, Churchill had said instead, "Well, men, just do your best. You probably can't sink it, but do your best."

Churchill closed all the escape hatches. He was 100 percent committed to sinking the Bismarck. And it was sunk.

---

[1] As reported in *Saturday Evening Post,* under the title, "The Last Nine Days of the Bismarck," November 15, 22, and 29, 1958.

You Can Apply Churchill's Formula

Application of the Churchill motivation formula to day-to-day situations gets big, surprising results. For example, an insurance executive in Hartford, Connecticut, credits the Churchill technique with helping him get twice the performance from his sales representatives.

After hearing me explain this method at a special seminar, this executive decided to apply it on telephone calls to his salesmen.

Below is his own description of what his phone calls sounded like *before* he put Churchill's technique to work.

THE USUAL APPROACH OF MEDIOCRE LEADERS
WEAK, INEFFECTIVE MOTIVATION

Bill: Hello Fred, this is Bill Thompson.

Fred: Hello, Mr. Thompson.

Bill: Say Fred, I'm calling to find out how things are going on the Smith deal. If possible, we need that account.

Fred: Well Bill, I'm doing all I can but there's a lot of competition. Frankly, I'm not optimistic.

Bill: I understand that. After all, I've been up against tough situations, too. And I admit competition is way up over last year.

Fred: Boy are you right on that! Not only is the Tennessee Company competing on this but so are two local outfits. It just doesn't look good.

Bill: Well Fred, all I can ask you to do is give it a try.

Fred: Thanks Bill, I'm glad you realize we can't win them all.

Bill: (Half-laughingly.) Well, just give it a good try. Let me know how it turns out. Goodbye.

Fred: Thanks a lot. Goodbye.

Now, contrast Bill Thompson's motivational technique *after* adopting Churchill's approach. Notice his positive, direct statements. Notice how the salesman is almost compelled by a powerful psychological force to succeed.

THE CHURCHILL WAY
STRONG, POWERFUL, COMPELLING MOTIVATION

Bill: Hello Fred, this is Bill Thompson.

Fred: Hello, Mr. Thompson.

Bill: Fred, I'm calling to remind you of your overriding responsibility to get that contract tomorrow.

Fred: Well, I'll do my best. But you know the Brown organization will be in there. And I just learned that the Tennessee Company is trying for it too. Now, we're at a pretty bad price disadvantage.

Bill: Fred, you have just one responsibility tomorrow. Get that contract. Are your charts ready? (Yes) What about the cost projections? (All ready, sir) Have you developed the special rider proposal? (It's ready).

Bill: Good. Now remember Fred, this can mark the turning point in our company. It is critically important. Nothing else should have any consideration whatever. You are to get this contract. Everything is on our side. Do you understand?

Fred: I'm ready, sir.

Bill: Fred, listen to me carefully. You can do it. You've got the advantages on your side. So, get that contract.

Fred: Very good, sir. I'll get it.

Bill: That's the spirit. Goodbye.

The Churchill Formula in a Nutshell

Here it is, step by step—a sure way to get larger results from people. Try it at work tomorrow. See how it promotes action, builds morale and gets positive results.

1. Define precisely the job you want done.
Churchill said: "Your job is to sink the Bismarck."

You say (examples): "Get the order from the X Company."

or

"Reduce costs by 10 percent."

or

"Get the report ready by 11 A.M."

2. *Don't leave any room for doubt.*

Churchill said: "No other considerations are to have any weight whatever."

You say (examples):   "This is an absolute necessity.
                                                or
                                "This is your prime responsibility."
                                                or
                                "This calls for a 100 percent maximum effort."

3. *Be sure all necessary preparations have been made.*

Churchill said: "You're taking every possible step to see the Bismarck is sunk?"

You say (examples):   "Have you got all your facts together?"
                                                or
                                "Have you gone over every detail?"
                                                or
                                "You're ready in every sense of the word?"

4. *Impress your people with immense importance of what they are to do.*

Churchill said: "Not only the possible steps, not only the easy steps . . ."

You say (examples):   "I don't care what it takes, get results."
                                                or
                                "Go after this with every ounce of energy you've got."
                                                or
                                "Leave nothing to chance. We've got to win this one."

5. *Insist, insist, insist on victory.*

Churchill said: "The eyes of the whole world are upon us."

You say (examples):   "Our company must have this business."
                                                or
                                "Everyone here is behind you 100 percent."
                                                or
                                "It's up to you now to come through."

Don't Be an "Other People Blamer"

Here's an infallible way to judge the psychological size of people: Watch them when something goes wrong and observe whom they blame—themselves or "other people."

Psychological dwarfs—the petty people who never move up to real success and never seem to achieve anything of significance invariably blame "other people."

Psychological giants, the leaders and big earners—the successful people—invariably blame themselves when something doesn't turn out right.

Please note this carefully: real leaders are not psychological escape artists. Big leaders live the philosophy "I Am The Captain of My Fate, I Am The Master of My Soul."

Below are several common situations. Note the difference between the point of view between the 100 percent responsible individual and the typical "someone else is to blame" person.

Situation	Typical "other people are wrong" person	Superior person who lives 100 percent responsible rule
1. Student receives low grade.	Blames the instructor (Was unfair. Likes to see students fail).	Blames himself. Didn't study hard enough.
2. Employee misses out on promotion.	Boss was either unfair or blind.	Thinks: "I'm deficient in some respect, I've got to take corrective action."
3. Motorist gets ticket for going 50 in 30 mile zone.	"Those cops ought to be solving crimes instead of hiding to catch guys like me."	"I got precisely what I deserved. I can't blame anyone but myself."
4. Minister finds attendance way off.	Blames congregation. "It's awful the way people put the church in second place."	"Something I'm doing is wrong. I'm not getting through. I've got to find a way to boost attendance."

| 5. Salesman misses out —loses to competition. | Explaining to sales manager, "It's simple. They have us beat on price," (or quality or delivery or some other logical basis). | Explain to sales manager "I messed up some way. Would appreciate your working with me to help me find out how." |

A friend explained it to me this way: "If people would just learn it only makes them look weak and small to pass the buck, maybe they would quit."

Sometimes I feel more mental energy is devised in trying to cover up tracks, protect oneself, develop an evacuation route, than is spent doing the work.

I've frequently observed a salesman I know, who has achieved a very mediocre record, spend more time planning his excuse for not making a sale than he invested in preparing to make the sale.

When you totally commit yourself to a project you harness all your psychological energy. But, when you have an escape hatch, only a portion of your energy is put to work. Result: either failure or mediocre performance at best. The schoolboy who says, "I can always drop the course if I don't like it," cuts down his mental efficiency by at least 50 percent. When he should be studying, he goofs off.

Become 100 percent committed if you want to win it.

IN QUICK REVIEW HERE'S HOW TO GROW A MENTAL FORT

1. Remember the Alamo. Block off all avenues to psychological retreat if you want to win.

2. In tough situations say, "I take full responsibility," and then watch yourself grow.

3. Apply the Churchill formula to get results from people. Don't give your subordinates a map for retreat. Give them a map for success.

4. Learn to blame yourself when things aren't going quite right. You'll find it pays.

How To Get Ahead
Faster
By Thinking
Bigger

7

What Comprises Real Beauty?

Ever ask yourself this question? Ever wonder why some women just seem to have that intangible but very, very real *"it"* while other women just plain don't excite any man let alone make other women envious?

Let me relate an incident which tells the most important beauty secret you will ever hear.

A few months ago I had a long, interesting chat with my mother about her "business" which she started when she was 64. Now past 73, Mother is having a wonderful time designing and making bridal gowns. Each dress is an exclusive. The challenge of originality plus the excitement of helping young, vibrant brides-to-be maximize their big moment give Mother a joyous and refreshing feel for life. Most women her age have spiritually passed on years and years ago.

She and I chatted about her chief interest—what it takes to make a bride attractive. She showed me dozens of pictures of "her" brides in their bridal costumes. And, what amazed me was that each of them *was* attractive. I half-way jokingly said, "Mother, don't you have any homely girls around here any more?"

She laughed, but then in a very serious and professional way answered, "Why, no. All women have beauty. All I have to do is find it. By that I mean I just have to design everything to bring out the natural beauty that's there.

"Here, let me show you," she went on, "look at this girl." I looked and saw a beaming, almost spellbinding bride. "Now, she came to me with a picture from a fashion magazine and told me that's the kind of dress she wanted. Well, the girl who modeled the dress for the magazine couldn't have weighed 100 pounds. But the girl who came to see me weighed at least 145.

"Here I had a problem," Mother explained. "I had to show her that the dress the model was wearing looked good on the model. But it wouldn't be best for her. After a while she understood and I designed the dress you see in this picture. The dress I designed shows up the best parts of her figure and de-emphasizes the others. I do the same thing with all of 'my' girls."

We continued to look through Mother's album of bridal pictures. She made comments as we went along explaining how she designed dresses to accentuate the beauty that is in each woman. Comments like, "This girl was flat-chested. Notice that I did this . . ." or "This girl's coloring was such and such so I did so and so," or "Now this girl was tall, even taller than her husband, so I shortened her like this . . ."

A Dynamic Beauty Secret

After a while Mother summarized her experiences this way: "I can't create beauty but I can find it and then bring it out. Most women, maybe 19 out of 20, make one basic blunder when they buy clothes or get their hair fixed or do anything else about their appearance. They copy each other too much. Each woman is different. The clothing, the hair arrangement, the make-up should all be chosen to bring out the best in the woman. Copying some other woman who may weigh 20 pounds more or less or be several inches shorter or taller or has a different bone structure, makes a lot of women look frightful."

Moral: A woman doesn't make herself beautiful by copying another woman. *Beauty, like success in all things, is individual.* The woman (and the man, too) who asks, "What is best for me?" is on the right track to better personal appearance.

Since that visit with Mother, I've been more aware of women and their beauty, or the reasons why they may lack it, than before. Many little incidents since have made me even more aware that "what's good for Betty may be completely wrong for Joan."

For example, very recently I was having lunch in a French restaurant with a business friend when two women took a table close to us. My friend glanced in their direction, then looked at me and said, "Doesn't that woman facing this way have her hair fixed beautifully?" I looked and agreed. She was wearing her hair in an old fashioned "bun" and it looked fine.

On the street a few minutes later I noticed another hair-do just like the one we both had admired in the restaurant. "What do you think of that woman's hair?" I asked, glancing to indicate the woman in mind. "Oh, gads! That's horrible, isn't it?" my companion replied.

And it was. But the hair-do we both found quite unattractive was the same style as we had both admired just a few minutes before. There was just one difference: the women.

The point restated: What is good for another person may not be good for you. Think: "What is best for me?" Then act.

Dare To Be Original

Now, let's leave appearance and test the validity of this success principle. Think: "What is best for me?" in other situations.

In a confusing world, it's easy to get all mixed up about some things. One of these is competition.

Have you ever noticed how often you hear someone say, "What is so and so doing about it?" or "What does he think?" or "How did they solve it?"

I once served on a college faculty committee set up to study the curriculum offered and then suggest any needed changes. The action of the committee soon took on the form of, "This is what they do at such and such a university so I think we ought to do it here too." The "research" of this committee consisted mainly of inspecting the catalogs of other schools to see what they were doing. The committee met, and met, and met some more.

Finally, after numerous meetings (usually late Friday afternoons) in which the committee did little more than argue about which of the leading schools should be imitated, one professor, who had grown quite exasperated, said, "What's good for Harvard or Illinois or Chicago may be good for them. But it may not be good for us. Our situation is different from all others. So why don't we think in terms of what's good for us, not what's good for them. Let them run their university and let us run ours."

The good professor opened the eyes of some of our colleagues that afternoon and the committee began to work constructively as builders, not as imitators.

Business consultants report the same disease, "copyitis", infecting otherwise fine corporate minds. Often, in every industry, we find companies that spend virtually all of their thinking time in studying how the competition is doing it. Sometimes a company duplicates the program of a competitor to such an extent that there really is no competition. There is just "copytition."

One executive in a leading bank talked with me on this point. He said, "We really have no competition. In our planning, we are concerned with what is best for us. Meanwhile our competition is trying to do exactly what we do. When we changed our advertising theme a few months ago, they picked it up right away. When we put out a premium offer, they were right behind us. But we were there *first*.

"Our competitors just prove to the public that we're right.

We are the originals. Our competitors are the carbon copies. If the day ever comes when our competitors go out on their own and do things we're not doing, *then* I'll have real cause for concern!"

In the mind of the buyer the imitators are saying, "Well folks, the leader is right. So we've decided to do just what he's doing. Since he did it first, better use his product. We may not have copied it exactly right."

People who win success in a big, big, way know it's foolish to just try and keep up with or beat someone else. People who arrive at big destinations get there by competing with themselves, their own abilities. They don't ask themselves, "Am I as good as Harry or George?" Instead they ask, "Am I operating at *my* full potential? Am I doing as good a job as *I* can?"

Do What Is Best For You

A merchant friend who has developed three profitable delicatessens explained his success to me this way. "In everything I do I just concentrate on what is best for my store. What will bring customers to me? I don't add a product just because the other stores around here add it. My store is different from their stores. Sure, I keep an eye on what they are doing, but I don't get all excited because they do something I don't do. I figure the best way to get ahead in business is to chart my own course and not move from it. The way I look at it, I'm not running their stores. I'm running mine.

"So many businessmen are so busy copying each other that they just don't make progress. To me competition doesn't mean doing the same thing as somebody else. Competition means doing something different and better. I don't want to be a 'competitor.' I want to be a leader."

The leader asks, "What is best for me?"

The second-rater asks, "What is the leader doing?"

Don't you see? You automatically lay claim to leadership

when you start thinking, "What is best for me?" instead of "What are the others going to do?" Success comes almost in proportion to your ability to stand out as an *individual*.

Consider what it takes to become a really top-flight, highly paid salesman. *Fortune* magazine some years ago did some research on the men who succeed in selling $1,000,000 worth of insurance in a single year.

The main conclusion *Fortune* reached was this: "It is highly doubtful if sales tactics, of themselves, account in any great degree for the outstanding successes in life underwriting." Why? Because among this very select group of salesmen were all types of men—men who were very extroverted and men who were quiet and reserved, men of all body builds, men of widely differing educational backgrounds, men of different interests. The one thing these men had in common was an *"almost fanatical belief in the virtues of insurance and the benefits it brings to the insured and to society."*

The million-dollar-a-year man was in short "a missionary."

Fortune went further to point out something exceptionally significant. The million dollar a year producers "are an interesting study of how individuals of contrasting backgrounds and temperaments can, by playing the game according to their separate lights and strengths, reach the same goal."

Again, "doing what's best for me" pays off in maximum achievement. Get used to the fact that you are different. And once you are used to it, capitalize on it.

Last January in Florida I met an old friend of mine, Harry Atkinson, who has developed quite a reputation selling industrial chemicals. Harry related an incident to me which drives home the power of originality and the dangers involved in copying someone else's approach.

"Let me give you a little background," Harry began. "As you probably guessed, in my dealings with people I'm not the conformist type. When I greet a customer I let him know with a good hard back slap or two that I'm really glad to see him. Why, I even cuss in a friendly sort of way at some of the people I call on."

"Sounds good to me if it gets you results," I injected.

"Well, it does," Harry continued. "I don't like phonies and I find being my natural self pays off. But I sure don't recommend my methods to other people."

"Why not?" I asked.

"Well," Harry went on. "Let me tell you what happened to me. A while back my Sales Manager hired a kid fresh out of college. The boss kept him around our Charlotte plant for about a month and then decided to put him in the field with an experienced salesman.

"Now, here's where the trouble started," Harry explained. "I told my Sales Manager not to send the boy out with me because I don't sell like the book says. But the Sales Manager insisted. He reminded me that I had the best record and he wanted this young fellow to learn from the best.

"Well, to make a long story short, the kid traveled the territory with me for 2 weeks. He'd watch my flamboyant methods and even though I told him to use his own techniques, he insisted on trying to copy me.

"Hell, it was so miserable it was funny in a way. He'd walk in and try this back slapping approach of mine and the customers would just about kick him out. Basically, the boy was quiet and reserved. He was completely out of place doing things my way."

"What finally happened?" I asked.

"Just exactly what you'd think," Harry answered. "The boy quit. He concluded that my way, which he just plain couldn't get used to, was the only way to sell. And since he couldn't do it my way he left and got himself some kind of office job.

"I hope," Harry concluded, "that you make one point crystal clear whenever you're talking to young salesmen."

"What's that?" I asked.

"Just this: make sure you tell them that anyone can be a terrific salesman if he'll just concentrate on developing the method which works best for him. And tell them also that as soon as they stop copying somebody else's technique they're automatically opening the door to really great performance."

Money Is Where You Find It

If you want to find oil, go where oil can be found. This sounds pretty obvious, doesn't it? If you really wanted to find oil, you would go where the odds are pretty good you could find oil.

Or if you wanted to catch fish, you sure wouldn't go someplace where there were no fish. And you may have observed that smart girls who are eager to find a man don't go to some isolated girls' school. No, they go to the State University where men generally outnumber girls.

But a funny thing happens when it comes to going after money. Unless we are schooled the right way, we almost instinctively go looking for money where money can't be found in desirable quantities.

I learned this lesson many years ago when I was in college. I needed more money. Making ends meet was pretty tough. About the best thing I felt I could do was sell Fuller brushes. A lot of young men still find this activity an excellent source of supplemental income.

Well, I got my samples, read the instruction book and was all set to go. And I guess I followed the course of action just about all beginning door-to-door salesmen follow. I selected about the most run-down neighborhood I could find and proceeded to sell.

It was no great problem seeing the people. There were lots of them. But what I soon discovered was that the area was overpopulated with rather special people—*other salesmen*. In fact, it got to look almost as if some blocks were being picketed. Many afternoons I would meet the same salesmen. We soon were calling each other by name. More than once I even was in a house with another salesman making a presentation at the same time to a homemaker.

Then there were other problems. When it came time to close the sale, there always was the problem of money. The homemaker would stall, telling me to come back on Saturday, or a week from Saturday, or a week from Friday, or Monday at 6:45, and then I could get my money.

Finally, a veteran salesman and business executive I chanced to meet took me aside and gave me one of the most striking lessons in Basic Economics I have ever learned.

"Look," he said, "do what I tell you and you will triple your income."

This, of course, interested me. (Doesn't making three times as much money with the same expenditure of effort interest you, too?)

Here's what he told me to do. "Go to the Upper Hilltop Section and just sell the same way you've been selling."

Now, I knew the Upper Hilltop Section was a high-income neighborhood so I protested. Like most people, I was afraid of the fine homes, nice cars, and the other obvious elements of success. But my "tutor" was firm. "I told you you'd make three times as much money. Now, if you don't like this idea, forget it."

I felt challenged to the point I had to try. And I soon found my advisor was right. I tripled my income the very first day! Here is what I discovered. First, there were almost no salesmen in this neighborhood. In the several months that I sold brushes I rarely encountered another door-to-door salesman selling anything.

Another thing I soon found out was that people in the higher income homes were much more approachable. They were easier to talk to, friendlier, less harried by the troubles of the world. And a third big thing I discovered was that money was no problem. I could collect on the spot and I could sell much more per order.

After two weeks of this new success, I called my friend to thank him for steering me straight. He chided me a little. "You surprise me. I thought they taught you logic at the University."

I explained that they did. And he replied with this: "Well, then, you ought to be able to figure this out. In the high-income area, there is five times as much money and only one-fifth as many salesmen. Boy, you should get rich."

I learned this lesson well. If you want to sell anything, go to people who have the money to buy.

You can check this quite easily. If you look around, you will find that there is far more competition to get the dollars of the low-income people than there is to get the dollars of the high-income people. It just doesn't make sense.

But a lot of the things people do don't make sense.

A friend of mine, who is very successful in the sale of printing, follows the same formula I learned in my door-to-door experience. "Most printing jobs," my friend explained to me, "involve between two hundred and five hundred dollars. And these jobs involve a whole lot of headaches. On the other side of the picture, perhaps 10 percent of the printing jobs involve an expenditure of at least one thousand dollars and often many thousands of dollars. Well, after I had struggled to make a living selling the little prospects, it hit me—why not go after the big dollar?

"Now, my experience shows this. I actually found less competition for the big customers than I did for the little customers. And I found it easier to deal with these people because when I sell printing involving several thousands of dollars, I generally work with someone in a customer's business who is responsible and thinks on a bigger scale. They don't try to shave every last dime off my price."

This change in philosophy certainly proved to be a big benefit to my friend. Today he has the 5 bedroom, 5 bath home, his own $90,000 airplane, five wonderful children, and a future that has no limits. It all began he said when he decided to stop "competing" for the little customer and concentrate on the big prospect.

My friend also carries this philosophy over in to the selection of his employees. "When I hire other salesmen now," he explains, "I look for a fellow who can think and communicate on a bigger scale. It doesn't take any more time and it doesn't involve any more trouble to go after the big order than it does to go after the little order. And there is definitely less competition!

I've seen exactly the same thing happen to salesmen who sell real estate. In the low and medium priced homes, there are perhaps five times as many salesmen as there are for the high priced homes. This reveals one basic fact about human nature. Most people are afraid to go after the big job, the big sale, the big order, the big career, the big anything. Because they feel inferior, they don't try.

An insurance executive I know answers the question, "How much money can I make selling life insurance?" in a classic manner. He asks the interested young man this, "How much money do your friends make?"

My friend has discovered after hiring hundreds of salesmen that their earning capability is about equal to that of the people with whom they feel comfortable. That is, if they feel at ease associating with $8,000 a year people, that's about how much they are going to make in the insurance business. But if they feel comfortable, can communicate, share the same interests, and aren't afraid of people earning $20,000, $30,000, and more per year, that's about how much they are going to make.

We catch the same kind of fish that we ourselves actually are. If we feel ill at ease with high income people, odds are that we'll never make the high income. Part of the solution here is to cultivate the ability to meet people and to understand people who live on a plane where we would *like to live*.

The Test of a Mature Person

A very successful executive friend of mine fell in love with growing exceptionally fine roses about 5 or 6 years ago. Like so many other leaders, he turns to nature for his relaxation and psychological refreshment.

One day, as he was discussing his latest find, a special rose imported from Australia, he went on to tell me of his pet peeve.

"You know, Dave, I really enjoy my roses," he said, "but lately I'm getting really teed off."

"Why so?" I asked.

"Well," he explained, "quite a few people stop by to see my roses. Now what disappoints me is that they can't appreciate roses for what they are, a beautiful flower. Instead they say something like, 'You ought to enter these in a contest,' or 'This one is even bigger than so and so's roses.'

"Heck, Dave," he went on, "what these pint-sized people can't get through their heads is that I'm not growing roses to prove I'm better than other people. I grow roses for my own selfish enjoyment, period."

My friend was really worked up. "I told my wife last night I'm going to declare the rose gardens and my green house off limits to everyone except my gardener if people won't stop telling me to enter some contest."

Before we changed the subject he added, "I grow roses because I like roses. It's that simple. I have no desire whatever to prove I can grow better roses than the people next door. To me, that's stupid. 'My roses are better than your roses,' is just a carry over from the 'my daddy can beat your daddy' attitude kids have."

There you have an example of full maturity. When we do things to please ourselves rather than to prove we're "better" than somebody else, then we're mature.

Now here's the startling difference. It's a gigantic difference. It's a difference which can remake your life and the lives of those you love if you will but learn it. Mark this point well: success-oriented people compete with their own potential; failure-oriented folks compete with other people.

I enjoy football. And the longer I've been interested in the game, the more my preference has drifted toward the professional teams. Why? The fellows in high school and college too often are playing mainly to be heroes. The fellows in the professional leagues are playing to get the most out of themselves.

Watch a pro miss a pass. *For a moment he hates himself. He doesn't hate the passer.* He hates himself for having goofed. This, right here, is a mark of the pro. In the amateur games, the fellow who misses the pass goes back to the huddle and chews out the passer—he blames someone else. *The pro blames himself.*

So it is in all fields.

Be jealous of your own potential, but never jealous of the performance of others.

Last month I was reading an article which compared the United States economy with that of a number of other countries.

The author was very pleased with our accomplishments. "The evidence clearly shows that we lead other countries in practically every department. For example, in the U. S. there are X phones per 1000 people while in China there are Y per 1000, and in Russia Z. There is no indication that these countries will overtake us in the foreseeable future."

Now, doesn't this approach disgust you? Frankly, to compare the U. S. economy with second and third rate economies is almost as foolish as comparing the prizefighting abilities of a Sonny Liston with Frank Sinatra! To sit back and relax because we have more planes or cars or beds or food than another country is surrendering to mediocrity, and at the same time, denying ourselves an even higher standard of living.

The point is this: when the United States competes with its own potential, then we will eat *even better*, sleep in *even better* beds, educate our children in *even better* schools, and own *even better* television sets.

Exactly the same point applies when you compete with your own potential rather than competing with second-raters who are near you.

Remember, the real pro always competes with himself.

What About This Conformity Business?

A little while back I read a magazine article about conformity in a large "middle class" suburb near San Francisco. It seems in this development there are several hundred houses all exactly the *same* size and the *same* design. The lawns are exactly *the same*. In each yard there is one tree planted at exactly the same place.

The people who live in these homes have surrendered to conformity to such an extent they organized a civic association to make sure no one plants a second tree or paints his house another color or does anything which would distinguish his house.

Well, it seems one fellow decided he was going to plant some ivy in his yard. But no sooner was this done than the civic association clamped down and brought legal action to compel him to dig up the ivy and plant the prescribed grass.

Now this is conformity and it illustrates a point which you can profit from!

Most "ordinary" or "average" people don't like the person who dares to be different. These conformists, and they are in the majority, feel uneasy when someone else expresses originality. So they fight it.

Remember this: The bottom group will fight you if you don't conform. But the top group will welcome you.

Birds of a feather *do* flock together. So, if you're in a situation where you feel pressure to conform, get out, and join the group that admires creativity.

You live in dangerous times. There is enormous pressure to standardize you. The little, petty, people in this world want you to do everything exactly like everyone else.

The rule is: Develop your own method. Perhaps this is the most difficult lesson of all to learn. Watch the star pitcher out there on the mound. His windup, his delivery are unique; his methods aren't copied. His method is *his* method perfected.

Or watch the pro golfer take his swing at the ball. He does it *his* way.

The prize-winning writer has perfected *his* style; the artist who reaches the top has perfected *his* method; the great public speaker has mastered *his* technique, *his* delivery.

Let me develop this point just a bit more. You can spend the rest of your lifetime looking at the other 2,999,999,999 people on this earth and you won't find anyone else who is exactly like you. You are different. You are unique. There is one of you. And there is *only* one of you. No one else has your peculiar abilities, your exact intelligence, your particular viewpoint.

When God made you he threw away the formula!

Now, if you have a complete grasp of this fundamental truth, you are prepared to take a giant step forward to better things, better times, more money, more happiness, more good. You are equipped to recognize several things:

No one else's methods are exactly right for you and copying these methods can lead you to mediocrity.

"Competing" with someone else, whether in social or business matters, can destroy your chances for maximum achievement.

The only answer is competition with the vast potential which is found in YOU.

PUT THESE IDEAS TO GOOD USE

1. All people can be attractive. But beauty or handsomeness is individual. Be Distinctive. Dress the way which is best for you.

2. Remember, most competition is really copytition. Real competition is working against your own potential. Copyitis will destroy you.

3. If you want to find money, go where the money is. There is 5 times as much competition for the money of people who have very little as for the money of people who have a lot. Go after big *customers,* big *opportunities,* big *success.*

4. Learn to be comfortable with people in the income bracket you want to join. If you can be comfortable, enjoy same interests, feel at ease with $50,000 a year earners, you've won half the battle in joining them.

5. Be jealous of your potential but never jealous of the potential of others.

How To Use Psychic Conditioning
To Get
Everything You Want
Out Of Life

8

Before you get into this chapter, make sure of one thing. Make certain you are open-minded and mentally receptive. Do this, because we are ready to explode an old myth, one which has helped guarantee failure and mediocrity for a long, long time.

This myth, put in only six words is: "Thinking does *not* make it so." It's wrong, stupid, foolish to believe it.

Achievement has always required a disciplined and controlled psyche. And basic to a managed psyche is full acceptance of this success-producing law: *Thinking DOES make it so.*

Let me warn you. Actually understanding, believing, and putting this concept to happiness-producing, money-making use is not easy. Perhaps it's because this fundamental truth is too simple. Perhaps it's because the environment around us is too negative, too failure-oriented to permit us to grasp this wisdom.

All I ask here is that you try.

To get started let's work through one basic situation. Let's take the formula *Thinking Does Make It So* and apply it to one facet of life. We'll take an assumed case but you can follow along and apply it to your situation. Let's assume Louise, a typical 35-year-old woman, is married to Fred, a typical 38-year-old man. OK? Now, without changing Fred one iota, let's see how Louise has it within her psychic power to prove Fred is a louse or prove Fred is an angel. Look at the diagram below.

Louise says mentally, "I choose to prove Fred is a louse. Here's why."	*Louise says mentally, "I choose to prove Fred is an angel. Here's why."*
1. "Fred doesn't tell me all that goes on at the office. I'm suspicious, very suspicious."	1. "Fred loves the kids—buys them too much I guess. But he can't help it."
2. "Last week he was out two evenings while I had to stay home with the kids. It's always like that."	2. "Fred lets me write all the checks. He never fusses at me about money."
3. "Fred likes his mother more than mine. He's very unfair."	3. "Fred is all man. He never goes around complaining like most men do."
4. "He doesn't appreciate me. He didn't even notice my new slacks."	4. "He always brings me a surprise when he comes home from a trip."
5. "Fred worries more about his business than he does about me."	5. "Fred never seems to care if the house is messed up. A lot of men do."
Louise is right: Fred is a louse.	*Louise is right: Fred is an angel.*

Note: In each instance, Fred is still exactly the same as he was before the psychic machinery was set in motion. In Louise's mind, Fred becomes what Louise *decides* he should become. Insofar as Louise is concerned, Fred is good or Fred is bad, depending on which Louise decides he should be.

In a phrase, *Thinking Does Make It So*. You can, if you wish, apply this psychic law to any situation you face. "Prove" your boss is a skunk and he is. Prove he's a wonderful guy and he is.

I covered the "Thinking *Does* Make It So" concept recently in a management seminar for senior executives. Afterward, one gentleman, who happened to own a machinery company, said to me:

"As you were talking you made me think of a problem we had in my business," he began. "I'd had my eye on a small plant in Virginia. Thought we might want to buy it and merge it with our company.

"Well," he continued, "I didn't want to make a commitment before I checked it out with my staff. So, I called in my two key men, Harry L., my Sales Manager, and John B., who is in charge of production. I filled them both in and said, 'Look, in a month, give me a written report on what each of you thinks we should do.'

"The reports came in right on schedule," my friend continued. "Dr. Schwartz, I wish you could have seen them. Harry, the Sales Manager felt we should go ahead. He had pages of advantages that showed how much more money we'd make. He was all go.

"But John took just the opposite view. His advice was, 'Stay out of it.' He built an air-tight case for not buying them out.

"Here," the executive continued, "you have a perfect case of two men, each pretty competent and each with the same facts, reaching completely different conclusions."

"Which one did you buy?" I asked.

"Well, I bought Harry's ideas. I don't know why except my intuition seemed to tell me it was the right thing to do."

"How's it working out?" I inquired.

"We've only had the plant for 9 months and we're already making money. We made the right choice all right."

There you have it. We prove what we tell our psychic machinery to prove. Thinking really *does* make it so.

Let's go ahead now and see how you can modify your psychic processes to get the kind of results you want.

Psychic Conditioner #1—THINK "I Feel Good" and you do

Let me tell you about a wonderfully inspiring experience that I witnessed one Sunday afternoon not long ago at the Indianapolis Airport. I was waiting to board my flight. Through the window beside my gate I could see two flight attendants preparing to lift a woman into the plane. She looked about sixty and was confined to a wheel chair.

She was badly crippled and required both men to lift her up the steps in her wheel chair. But I wish you could have seen her face. She was smiling, laughing, and acted as if this were the biggest adventure in her life. Her family was on the observation deck watching as she was being lifted into the plane. She waved with one arm and, following her feminine instinct, used the other arm to try to keep her dress from blowing over her knees.

Later aboard the aircraft I sat beside her and we had a wonderful 70-minute chat until I had to get off the plane in Atlanta. We never talked about her legs. I didn't learn why she was crippled. But I did learn she is tremendously happy. During the flight our conversation ranged from her children and her grandchildren to the problems the free world faces today to how we can strike a blow against juvenile delinquency. These are the things we talked about.

I make it a practice when aboard a plane to engage in conversation with the person sitting with me. But in flying a million miles I have never had a more enjoyable or positive companion. It was obvious by her actions, by her smile, by her attitude, that she was not going to let a severe physical ailment put her in a psychological grave. She was set to live. She had that "I feel good" feeling.

How did she do it? Without making a big ado about it she did it by counting her blessings over and over and over again. She counted the blessings of fine grandchildren. She counted the blessings of healthy, intelligent children of her own. She counted the blessings of expert physicians who helped her live. She counted the blessing of a friendly airline that expressed so much courtesy in the way they transported her aboard. These were blessings. Here was a lady crippled beyond repair who truly practiced the great philosophy, "I *choose* to feel good."

Prove It To Yourself

Here's a prank you can play. Perhaps it isn't a very nice game, but it does illustrate a point. Pick a good sport for the victim. And be sure this friend is someone with good "snap back" ability.

Then line up three other friends to cooperate with you.

Next, arrange things so each of you will see the "victim" alone but in quick succession on the same morning. Instruct each of your friends to make a big point out of how sick the victim looks— things like, "Gads, you look *awful* today. You must be sick." "Looks like you've got the flu." "Got a high fever? You look like you'd better see a doctor fast."

Done in serious, convincing fashion, the victim of your prank will actually be sick.

Remember, the power of suggestion works. The same idea repeated over and over again takes on the form of reality. Tell yourself, "You're poor," listen to other people tell you you're poor, live around other people who are poor and, friend, you become psychologically destitute!

An old college friend of mine likes to tell this story. To earn room and board at college Jim tended the old coal furnace and did other odd jobs for an elderly lady who lived alone in a big old house. The old woman frequently had trouble sleeping. When this happened, she'd take a sleeping pill. One night, as Jim relates it, the old woman knocked on his door and said, "Jim, I hate to bother you but I can't sleep and I'm out of sleeping pills. Do you have any?"

Now, Jim even then was a very enterprising fellow. So he

replied "I sure do Mrs. B, but mine are downstairs. I'll go get one for you."

Then Jim rushed downstairs, went to the pantry and got a big lima bean.

He knew Mrs. B had very poor eyesight, and couldn't tell the difference between a lima bean and an oval-shaped sleeping pill. So, back upstairs, he said, "Now this is an extra *large* sleeping pill. It really works. Take it and you'll go right to sleep."

The old woman took the "pill" and guess what happened? She had the soundest sleep of her life. From then on she continued to pester Jim to give her more of his "special" pills.

A suggestion planted in the mind grows. If it's a negative psychic seed, it grows negative fruit. But if it's a positive psychic seed, it yields positive fruit. "Fred, you look sick" will make Fred feel worse but "Fred, you look wonderful" makes Fred feel better.

Create the Air, "I Feel Great, Really Great."

Chances are before lunch and certainly before dinner tomorrow you will hear not one but several people tell you in one way or another how bad they feel. Some will complain about "the aches"—headache, backache, stomach ache, side ache. Some people will complain about other miseries ranging from, "I'm overworked," to "I'm exhausted," to "I don't feel good."

When you think about it a little, it becomes obvious that most people "don't feel good." But, then, most people aren't leaders. It is a habit of mediocrity to complain about "how bad I feel." It is a habit of leadership to stress "how good I feel."

Now let's go through this "I feel bad business" in slow motion. Suppose you meet someone today and in the early part of your conversation you say something like, "I feel awful, simply awful." What have you done? You've lowered your leadership quotient four ways:

1. You say in effect, "I want sympathy." But people don't like sympathy-seekers.

2. You focus attention on yourself when, as a leader, you should instead focus attention on the person to whom you are talking.

3. You become a pain symbol, something to avoid. Telling others about how bad the world is treating you passes on to them some of your psychological pain, and they don't like this. The ancient Greeks developed the philosophy that in life we strive to find pleasure and avoid pain. Now, many people are unconscious of how painful they are. They complain about their aches so much other people want to avoid them.

4. You actually feel worse. Just saying, "I feel bad" actually makes you feel worse.

Suppose that instead of telling another how miserable you are you said something like, "I feel wonderful, just wonderful today." You would have raised your leadership quotient because:

1. You are a symbol of pleasure, good times, prosperity. People like this and will enjoy being close to you.

2. You actually feel better. Just repeating, "I feel great" at each opportunity makes you feel better. This is auto-suggestion in action.

Cheer Up Someone Else

One secret to feeling better is to make someone else feel better. Many people grow glum—and frankly troublesome—when sick because they dwell solely on their own problems. I know one elderly lady, chronically ill with a stroke, who has become a terrible burden on her daughter. This woman is concerned solely with *her* problem. And because of this selfish self-interest she suffers much more than she would have to. True, she can't remove her physical pain, but she can lighten it by thinking about other people.

Now, are you agreed that the air "I feel great, really great" wins friends, makes those around you feel warmer, more responsive? The next step then is to learn how to feel great, really and truly great.

Psychic Conditioner #2—THINK "I Choose to Be Happy," and you are

Happiness, it seems, is something just about everyone wants but few "find." Some people, in fact, believe it's foolish to even want to be happy. One well-educated but bitter cynic told me not long ago, "This happiness business is just so much nonsense. If you take a realistic look at this world, there's nothing to be happy about.

"Only two kinds of people have a chance at happiness," he continued. "The first is like that fellow over there (here he pointed to a man who was loading garbage onto a truck). Now that lame-brain has no responsibilities, no education, no worries. He can be happy because he doesn't know any better. He hasn't got enough brains to know only fools can be happy.

"Now the other kind of person who can be happy," he went on, "is the loonie, the fellow whose thinking processes are totally disrupted. He can be happy."

That's a pretty sad point of view, isn't it? According to his philosophy, you've got to be either a near moron or insane to be happy. But the cynic is right on one score if what we see and hear happening is any measurement of happiness. A quick look at the front page of a newspaper tells you the world is full of problems—wars, strikes, threats of wars, human conflicts, storms, and maybe a couple of murders, suicides, or rapes thrown in for good measure.

And if you were invisible and could look in on the homes up and down your street and across your community, you'd find dis-appointingly little happiness. Fusses and feuds and arguments of varying intensity and over a variety of matters are the rule, not the exception.

Yet, all these people claim they would like to "find" happiness.

Right there—in trying to "find" happiness—is the explanation why so little exists. Hunting for happiness in far-away places, new people, larger bottles, is unrewarding. Nor is happiness something natural that comes and goes like the sunshine. And here is real news for you. You have about as much chance of stumbling into happiness as you have of inheriting a million dollars from a relative you didn't know you had.

A lot of folks have developed the "after" theory of happiness. According to the "after" line of reasoning, happiness comes after—*after* your work load gets lighter. *After* you get out of some difficulty. *After* you finish school or *after* you get promoted.

But, like tomorrow, "after" never comes.

Happiness, if we are to experience it, must come "now" and from things which make up "now." To state it more precisely, happiness—and sadness—is manufactured. Your psychic machinery makes happiness or sadness. If you want to be happy you must decide boldly and frankly, "I choose to be happy right now." Again, condition your psyche. Prove to yourself you are happy and you are. Here are two things to do which will help.

First, develop a list of reasons why common sense tells you you should be happy. Then review this list, and add to it, several times daily.

Each of us has his own special reasons why he should be happy, but here are five. Some of these apply to you, perhaps some don't. It's best to make up your own list. But here's a start:

1. I'm happy because of my children. They need me very much. Their future happiness depends on me.

2. I'm happy because of my health. I'm no perfect specimen but there are many, many who are less fortunate than I.

3. I'm happy because I've got a job, a chance to earn a living. I'm happy because I'm needed.

4. I'm happy to be alive in these exciting times. I'm fortunate. I could have lived in a different time period.

5. I'm happy because tomorrow will be a bright new day, as new and fresh as anything can be.

When you feel like feeling sorry for yourself because the world is miserable, just concentrate on the reasons why you're
6

happy. Say to yourself, "I choose to be happy. Here's why..."
Develop reasons why you are really glad to be alive.

The second step is this: Make thinking "I'm happy" a habit!
Make it second nature to feel great. Review your list first thing in
the morning. Check it again at noon. Go over it again after work
when that physical letdown may give you a mental letdown.

And be sure to meditate on your "Why I'm Happy" check-list
before you go to bed. Think happy thoughts before you go to
sleep and be refreshed. What you think about before you go to
sleep is the "gas" your mental motor runs on while you're asleep.
Put high octane thoughts into your mental engine and let it purr
along quietly and peacefully. Remember, the mind never stops.
Put quality materials into it during your conscious moments and
it will work for you efficiently during your subconscious moments.

Develop the "I feel great, really great" habit and watch your
leadership quotient shoot up.

It's really simple: Make the decision, "I choose to be happy."
Then (a) develop reasons why you should be happy, never once
thinking about the negatives, and (b) practice thinking "I'm
happy" until it's a deep-set habit.

Psychic Conditioner #3—THINK, "I choose to think I'm rich," and you are

The thing which defeats so many of us is we think poor instead of thinking rich. A while back a young life insurance salesman came to see me with his problem. He had built up an exceptional first year record but had gone into a severe, prolonged
slump.

What was wrong? It seems this fellow had become very depressed and worried about his future. He just knew he was going
to fail. His bills were mounting yet his commission checks were
almost nil.

He found himself in a situation which is so common in selling:
the more he needed the commission, the harder it was to earn it.

The more desperate he became, the harder it was to make the sale.

At one point in the interview he commented, "Why, Dr. Schwartz, I've even begged people to buy a policy. That's how desperate I am."

What happened is that this very promising young man had allowed poor thoughts to dominate his psyche. He was a self-made victim of poverty thinking.

I soon recognized that the key here was to get this fellow to start thinking prosperity and stop thinking poverty. I got him to see two things. First, that thinking "I'm poor," "I'm broke," "I'm headed for even worse poverty" leads straight to failure and the psychological poor house. Next, I caused this young man to *convince himself* that, even though he was financially almost broke, he was rich in what really counts. Over and over in many different ways I caused him to think "I'm rich in ability," "I'm rich in ambition," "I'm rich in opportunity," and "I'm rich in family love."

The result was almost fantastic. In less than a week he had written five applications for $165,000 coverage. He was again back on the high road.

I remember this incident so well for about a year later he came back to see me. "I want to show you something," he said as he untied a package. "Look what I've had framed to put in my office."

Here's what the framed message said:

I'M RICH!!!

I'm rich in ability
I'm rich in ambition
I'm rich in opportunity, and
I'm rich in family love.

Isn't this a different approach! My young friend had learned the critical lesson. Thinking rich leads to riches; but thinking poor leads to poverty.

You can check this for yourself. Try to find one successful person who does not think prosperity. And try to find a failure who doesn't think poverty.

The road to riches is paved with rich THINKING.

Some time ago I was relaxing in a hotel suite with a friend, a prosperous fellow who has far-flung business interests. We had known each other for several years and our conversation took a turn as to what makes some men succeed and others just crawl along.

My friend made an observation which I think will interest you. Here is what he told me: "I discovered years ago that prosperity begins with a prosperous attitude.

"You know, Dave," he said, "looking back I have to thank my mother for this prosperity attitude. You see, I was never allowed to think we were poor, although looking back when we were kids I can see now we barely had enough money to get by on. But mother never let us think we were poor.

"Once when my brother and I wanted to go to see a ball game, instead of saying, 'We can't afford it,' mother came up instead with a better idea. 'Why not get some of the boys together and let's go to the schoolyard and play we're the Yankees!'

"That's the way it always was. I'll never forget the time my sister had a big dance coming up. There was no money to buy a new dress. But mother didn't say, 'We can't afford a dress,' or 'You don't need a new dress,' or 'You will have to get by with an old one,' or as some mothers say today, 'You expect too much.' Instead mother agreed. I'll always remember what she said: 'You do need a new dress, but you deserve something even better than the ones in the store. Let's go out and get the material and I'll make one which is just right for you.'

"That's the way we grew up. When we didn't have money—which was just about all the time—my mother would always substitute something *even better*. It never really occurred to me I was poor. I always felt rich."

My friend paused for a moment, looked across the room and said, "You know, the worst thing about being poor is knowing it. My mother was very smart. Instead of building up an inferiority complex in me because we didn't have money, my mother built up a feeling of being rich in ways other than money—rich spirit, rich friends, rich opportunity.

"By the time I was ready for college, I *wanted* to work my way through and since I did not feel second class because I was one of the few students working, I was accepted by other young people who had far more money than I.

"Making money since college has been easy for me and I really think it's because I never build up an inferiority feeling about not having money."

There you have it. Pride, real bona fide self-respect, is the basic ingredient of all riches, including money.

A lot of problems are being created for the next generation right now by letting children feel they are poor. The amount of money available to spend on and for the children is not the criterion. The desirable thing here is never let the youngster feel poor.

There is a world of difference between "being poor" and not having money. When one has nothing but a poor feeling, continued poverty is the ultimate result.

How To Get the "Think Rich" Point of View

1. When you want to do something but don't have the money, substitute something else instead, and double your effort to have even more fun.

2. Count your other riches. Remember, if you are rich in desire, rich in ambition, rich in spirit, then other riches will automatically come to you if you cooperate.

3. And very important. Visualize yourself as having a substantial sum of money. Select a specific dollar goal and let this goal dominate your thinking.

4. Instead of wishing you had more money, instead of feeling sorry for yourself that you haven't got enough, buckle down, apply yourself, and set about making money.

5. Never, absolutely never, let yourself think you haven't got

what it takes to have more money. Remember the basic ingredient of monetary riches is first of all a rich spirit.

Think rich! Stop thinking poor!

Place a Value on Yourself—A High Value

Successful people place a high value on themselves. Once William Faulkner explained why he quit working in a post office. "Why should I be at the beck and call of anyone who happens to have three cents for a stamp?" Armed with the upgraded opinion of himself, Mr. Faulkner went on to become one of America's most respected writers.

Ask yourself, "Am I using me at my highest capacity?" If you get anything but a 100 percent positive answer, make the necessary changes.

The first step in developing money riches is thinking rich.

Look at it this way. The thoughts which buzz around in your mind all day are your voltage regulators. If these thoughts are poor thoughts like, "I'm not good enough to get the job I want," or "I'll always be poor," or "There are too many other people better qualified than I," then you're destined to have little. You might as well get used to the mud of mediocrity because you're stuck until your *thinking* changes.

But substitute positive, high-voltage thoughts like, "I'm the best qualified individual I know," or "I'm going to make money," or "I'm going to aim higher,"—then you *are* headed up.

Put differently, rich thinking makes rich bank accounts!

Create the Air "I'm in Demand. My Time Is Valuable."

One day about a week before Christmas several years ago I was standing on a corner just across from Rich's, the famous Atlanta department store. Hundreds of people were pushing their way in and out of the store each minute. I said to the fellow standing close to me, who also appeared to be waiting for someone, "I wonder why so many people shop at Rich's?" He turned, shifted the packages he was holding and said, "Well, I reckon the reason so many people shop at Rich's is because so many people shop at Rich's." I replied with an expressionless, "Oh," and we parted.

It was one of those phrases that immediately clings to your mind, "The reason so many people shop at Rich's is because so many people shop at Rich's." The more I went over it, the more it seemed to be a pearl of wisdom. (You re-read it a few times and see if you don't think it's pure, unadulterated wisdom.) The old fellow was so right. People go where there is a crowd. People go where other people go.

The businesses and the people who are most in demand are those who appear to be most in demand. This isn't double talk. This is Class A preferred common sense. Create an air of personal prosperity, of being wanted, and your popularity increases. The weakest selling appeal ever devised is the poverty approach, "I'm poor. Give me some business." Begging never develops business, it drives it away.

Create an air of being "hard up" and "I'm not doing so well," and you'll do worse. People love to do business—all kinds of business—with people who are in demand.

The Dean of Women at a State University in the Midwest told me an interesting case history as follows:

It seems a sophomore coed in this university had a problem not uncommon among coeds, dating. This girl was no candidate for campus beauty queen but she was an intelligent, pleasant girl. And she was on a campus where boys outnumber girls 2 to 1.

The young coed worried a lot about her lack of dates and her unpopularity. Finally she took her problem to the housemother of her sorority. Her housemother listened carefully and then said to her, "I'll tell you a secret technique that will greatly improve your popularity index. It will take a month perhaps, but if you'll give it time the results will be amazing."

The coed eagerly asked, "Tell me, I'm ready to try anything."

"Just this," replied the housemother. "There's a surplus of

young men on this campus and the social season is just getting started. You're almost certain to be invited out soon. But when you are, turn the invitation down."

"What!" asked the coed.

"Turn it down. And turn down all dates for the next month, all of them. Tell the young men you're already dated up."

"Hide if you must. But let everyone think you're the most popular girl here."

By the end of the month the girl's phone was ringing almost constantly. The coed learned that the girl most popular is the girl who is busiest. Young men don't want to date the girls other young men don't want to date. Young men want what they can't have. They want to date the busy girl.

Young physicians frequently experience difficulty in building a practice—the reason, of course, being that people are naturally just a little reluctant to turn over their health to someone inexperienced and unproved. A young doctor friend told me how an odd experience boosted his popularity.

"I had been in this town about a month. Only a handful of patients had visited me and these were suffering only from the most routine ailments. But things quickly changed for the better after a Friday night high school football game."

"Why," I asked, "were the teams that banged up?"

"Not at all," he laughed. "Here's what happened. A friend of mine from med school passed through town that night. Meanwhile, I had driven to another city on personal business and for some reason I'll never know, I neglected to tell my wife.

"Well, my friend, after talking with my wife and knowing that I liked football, just assumed I was at the game. So he called the stadium and asked that I be paged. I was—three times, as a matter of fact, and in a way that appeared to be a matter of great urgency.

"The next week I treated twice as many patients as in the first four weeks combined! When people learned I was in demand, my practice was assured."

People rush to buy from *busy* stores; people clamor to get on waiting lists at a *busy* physician's office; fellows fight to date the always-all-dated-up girl; people stand in line to eat in *busy* restaurants. People go where there is activity; people want what other people are enjoying.

Here is a suggestion for increasing your popularity and influence over people. Create an air of personal prosperity. Create the air, "I'm rich in customers," or "I'm rich in clients," or "I'm rich in admirers,"—whatever it is you want more of, convey the impression you already have lots of it. Create an air of personal prosperity and your prosperity will increase; but create an air of "I'm not doing so well," and you're sure to do worse. Prosperity begets prosperity; poverty begets poverty.

Proof That Self-Respect Is Enough

Many years ago I enjoyed a remarkable experience that demonstrated the power and value of self-respect. I arrived in a small Mississippi town where I was to spend one year. I inquired about living quarters from some of the local business citizens. One fellow suggested I go see "Miss Betsy, who has that big old house two blocks past the library on top of the hill."

"Of course," I was warned, "Miss Betsy is mighty finicky and she may not want you to live with her." (Later the meaning of that remark soaked in when I learned Miss Betsy had turned away dozens of people in the past because they weren't "quite right.")

Miss Betsy's house was a huge and bona fide old Southern mansion but now it was in a shabby, obviously run down condition. But the upper floor of the old mansion was clean and spacious, and I liked it. And Miss Betsy liked me so I moved in.

The remarkable thing about Miss Betsy was this. She had come from a wealthy, very cultured family. And until 20 years ago she had been wealthy. But virtually all her money was gone. She was, financially, poor. But at the same time she was rich in spirit.

Miss Betsy still played bridge each week with her three lady friends (all of whom were still wealthy). Miss Betsy still went to the same church (which was known as the rich folk's church). Miss Betsy still maintained the respect of business people in town.

She hadn't rented part of her house. Instead she "invited" that young professor to "stay" with her because she needed "young company." Everyone showed utmost respect for Miss Betsy because Miss Betsy respected herself.

One time I chanced to hear Miss Betsy's maid, who came in twice a week, tell someone at the door, "Miss Betsy ain't got no money no more but she sure ain't poor folks."

A superficial person might say, "Why doesn't that old woman salvage what she can and go live in an old people's home?" But Miss Betsy wasn't the surrendering type. Down deep Miss Betsy knew that the one most precious possession is self-respect and by preserving her self-respect she still had all the essentials of good living: friends, admiration, and acceptance.

What Determines How Much You're Worth?

After a training session a few weeks ago, a young man came to see me and asked if he could talk with me for a few minutes. I knew that this young fellow, now about 26, had been a very underprivileged child. On top of this, he had experienced a mountain of misfortune in his early adult years. I also knew that he was making a real effort to prepare himself for a solid future.

Over coffee, we quickly worked out his technical problem. Our discussion turned to how people who have few physical possessions should look toward the future. His comments provide a straightforward, sound answer.

"I've got less than $200 in the bank. My job as a rate clerk doesn't pay much and it doesn't carry much responsibility. My car is four years old and my wife and I live in a cramped, second-floor apartment with our year-old child.

"But Professor," he continued, "I'm determined not to let what I haven't got stop me."

That was an intriguing statement so I urged him to explain.

"It's this way," he went on, "I've been analyzing people a lot lately and I've noticed this. People who don't have much look at themselves as they are *now*. That's all they see. They don't see a future, they just see a miserable present.

"My neighbor is a good example. He's continually complaining about having a low-pay job, the plumbing that's always getting fouled up, the lucky breaks somebody else just got, the doctor bills that are piling up. He reminds himself so often that he's poor that now he just assumes that he's always going to be poor. He acts as if he were sentenced to living in that broken-down apartment all the rest of his life."

My friend was really speaking from the heart and after a moment's pause he added, "If I looked at myself strictly as I am— old car, low income, cheap apartment, and hamburger diet—I couldn't help but be discouraged. I'd see a nobody and I'd *be* a nobody for the rest of my life.

"I've made up my mind to look at myself as the person I'm going to be in a few short years. I see myself not as a rate clerk, but as an executive. I don't see a crummy apartment. I see a fine new suburban home. And when I look at myself that way I feel bigger and think bigger. And I've got plenty of personal experiences to prove it's paying off."

Isn't that a splendid plan for adding value to oneself? This young fellow is on the expressway to really fine living. He's mastered this basic success principle: *It isn't what one has that's important. Rather, it's how much one is planning to get that counts.*

The price tag the world puts on us is just about identical to the one we put on ourselves.

**Psychic Conditioner #4—THINK,
"Things will get better," and they do**

One mistake I've found a lot of people make in business is this: they think the world of economics is run by logic.

It's not. Business is guided only a little bit by logic and a whole lot more by psychology. Put this one in your success notebook right now.

A friend of mine, Hal Swift, a famous dance band leader of 20 years ago who is now a top earning apparel salesman, related an experience to me just recently which illustrates this point.

"I belong to a big trade show," Hal began. "We invite apparel retailers from many states to attend the market, see the merchandise and place orders. Well, last May our promotion committee decided to invite a well-known marketing authority to give a speech to the retail buyers attending the show. We really promoted the professor's talk because we felt he would have some good ideas on how to stimulate more sales.

"Brother, were we in for a shock!" Hal exclaimed. "The professor got up there and started talking about the possible danger signals of a new recession. He was equipped with all kinds of statistics about income, employment, trends, all that sort of thing and all of it bad. Hell, no one was even thinking of a business turndown until he harped away on it."

"What happened?" I asked, expecting the worst.

"Exactly what you'd expect," said Hal. "The retailers were nervous—scared is a better word. I think without a single exception, every retailer at this show bought less than he had planned. Business was off more than 30%. You could just feel the pessimism in the air. And all because some guy preached fear instead of optimism."

"Well," I said, "that sure does illustrate the point that bad news produces bad results."

"But wait," Hal broke in, "I'm not finished yet. It hurt all the other salesmen and it hurt me temporarily. But I got to work and did something to bring back optimism to my customers. Two days later I had a postcard printed and mailed it to all my customers who were at the show. Here, I've got one with me."

I looked at the card. It said: "Dear Customer: I disagree with the good professor. People are buying my line like crazy. Business has never been so good. P. S. I'll be calling on you in a couple of weeks to get the *rest* of your order. I know you didn't buy enough," signed Hal.

"It was amazing," Hal explained, "the card plus the optimism I always project got them back in a buying mood. I broke all my old records for the season."

We always get what we think. Think gloom, discouragement, poverty, and we get poorer. Think optimism, growth, prosperity and we get richer.

That's a law of the psyche.

Since When Is a Bird in the Hand Worth Two in the Bush?

For a number of years now I've stayed at a small, quiet hotel in the fifties when I'm in New York. I stay there because I can get maximum rest to recuperate from my always-too-full schedules.

And after a few stays at this hotel, it was natural that I should get to know the night manager, Herb L. Herb in many ways is a surprising fellow. He's about 60, exceptionally well-mannered, competent, and quite intelligent. (On different occasions late at night, I've found him reading such books as *War and Peace, Atlas Shrugged,* and *The Age of Reason,* all books which give anyone's brain a little workout.)

One evening I returned to the hotel about midnight after fulfilling a speaking engagement. Herb was in a talkative mood, and since I was really physically exhausted I was in a listening mood. It was a perfect conversational situation. Herb wanted to talk and I wanted to listen.

Herb was really disturbed, disturbed as are many people his age who feel they've somehow missed out on a lot of good, exciting living.

Herb began by saying, "You know, Dr. Schwartz, I really envy you making so many talks."

"Why so?" I asked, for it's rare for anyone on the public speaking circuit to be envied.

"Well," he explained, "you have a chance to help people straighten out their thinking before they get themselves so fenced in with the problems of life they can't escape.

"Every day I see people worshipping the God of Security when they ought to be worshipping the God of Adventure. If only someone had got me straightened out."

Herb went on to explain in some detail how he had started work in that very hotel as a bellman in 1928. He had big plans then, wanted to get in the securities business. But the great depression hit.

"New York was terrible in the early thirties, just terrible," Herb emphasized. "I felt so fortunate to have a job. And I was scared. As good times came back I played down my desire to get into some business which had a promise of a real future and more money. Well, to make a long story short, I stayed here because here I had security. Outside I felt I didn't.

"I guess I remembered too well the old saying '$50 a week for sure is worth more than $100 maybe.'

"Well, the thirties drifted into the forties. And the forties soon became the fifties. Now, we're well into the 1960's and I've passed the point of no return."

Herb paused a moment, then clenched his fist and hit the top of his desk with all the force he had.

"Oh, how I wish I'd gotten out and tried!"

"I hope," Herb concluded, "that you really make it clear to people that security is not the goal of life. Tell them the more they want security the less of everything else they're going to have."

As Herb was talking I remembered what a young fellow had told me during World War II. He elected to stay in the service for, as he put it, "I'll always have three squares a day and no worries." This fellow, who worshipped what Herb appropriately called the God of Security incidentally ended up with a self-inflicted wound fifteen years later.

Herb's problem is not rare, it's as common as mosquitoes. Herb failed to condition his psyche. Herb thought poverty. He failed to think optimism. Result: a man who lost out to his own negative thinking.

There are a lot of Herbs all around us, people who believe things will get worse instead of better. And for them, things always do get worse.

Psychic Conditioner #5—THINK, "It's a Good World," and It Is!

Remember the wise old man beside the road? Perhaps you remember the story of the old man beside the road who was visited by two strangers. It's one of my favorites for it tells so much about psychic conditioning.

It seems that this old man was sitting on the outskirts of a small town. A stranger drove up, opened the window, looked at the old man and said, "Old man, what kind of a town is this? What are the people like? I'm thinking of moving here."

The old man looked at the stranger and replied, "What were the people like in the town you just left?"

The stranger looked at the old man and says, "The town I just left had mainly pretty bad people. We just weren't happy there. People were just no good. That's why we're thinking about moving to this town."

The old man looked directly at the stranger and said, "Well, sir, I'm afraid you are out of luck because that's exactly the kind of people we have in this town."

A little while later another stranger drove up and asked the old man the same questions. "What kind of a town is this? What kind of people live here? We're trying to find a town to settle down in."

Again, the old man asked the question, "Well, what kind of people lived in the town from which you just came?"

The stranger answered, "Well, the people there were awfully nice. My wife and kids had a real good time living there, but I'm looking for a town where there's more opportunity than the one where we have been living. I sure hate to leave but we've no choice."

The old man said, "You're in luck, young man. That's exactly the kind of people we have here. You'll really like them and they'll like you."

The moral: *we find exactly what we seek.* If we are looking for bad people, that's what we'll find. If we are looking for good people, that too is what we'll find. Either way we see exactly what we want to see.

One morning a few years ago I was driving my son, David, to school. It was a rainy, relatively cold day. The radio was tuned to the news and weather station. The weather man was saying, "Sorry, folks, but we've got bad weather in store for you today. And to make things even worse, we hold *no hope* for any relief in the next 48 hours. It's going to continue to be damp, cold, and unpleasant. It may freeze and if it does, we're in for *real* trouble . . ."

When he finally finished, David, who was about 9, turned to me and said, "Dad, why doesn't that man let us decide what kind of a day it is? I thought it was pretty exciting but hearing him almost makes me feel we ought to stay home and go to bed."

David didn't know it was a "bad" day until the bad weather man started to sell bad weather.

Kids never complain about the weather. They don't differentiate between so-called "good" and "bad" weather until the weather men, parents, and other adults teach them to be prejudiced. Kids love all kinds of weather—hot, cold, dry, wet, cloudy, sunny—they love all of it until we poison their thinking.

Between now and tomorrow at this time, 5500 Americans will go to sleep for the last time. Think of it. Every day 5500 people, enough to populate a good-sized small town, are taken away by death.

This illustrates again how precious life is. Today, we consider 70 to be the life expectancy. Counting every one of them, that's

25,567 days. Certainly, we're not given enough time to waste it in worry, self-depreciation, gloom, and despair. Life is short, too short to spend it moaning and groaning.

Take time now to review yesterday. Ask yourself, "How would I have lived yesterday if I had thought in the morning this could be the last one?" How would yesterday have been different?

Here's a little guide to help. Equipped with "This Could Be the Last One" thinking, ask,

1. What kind of dinner would I prepare for my husband?
2. How would I react to my wife's dinner?
3. Would I scold the children for dragging in a little mud?
4. Would I have worried about money or promotions or other things?
5. Would I have lost my temper?
6. Would I have been disgusted with the weather?

It's good to re-examine each day. It's good to remind yourself, "This could be the last one," and then live accordingly. Remember, today, this very day, was the last day for 5500 people in the United States. When we realize just how fortunate we are to have this extra day, we avoid doing so much that only leads to heartache, disappointment, and sadness.

Every day is a bonus since no day is guaranteed.

Think about it this way: the child who goes to the state fair with $2 will think much more carefully about how to spend the $2 than the child who has $1,000 to spend. The trouble is, too often we live like the second child. We squander instead of choosing carefully.

Not long ago after I gave a talk to a group of building supply wholesalers, one fellow remained to chat. "I can see how your philosophy on psychic control would have worked 40 years ago. But I think it's unfair to think it will work today."

I, of course, asked why. (Don't misunderstand. I still run into more than my share of pessimists. But the evidence to support "psychic control" is so overwhelming I find it almost impossible to imagine anyone being a doubter.)

"Well," he explained, "today things are different. The really good days are gone. Why, any day we could be cremated in a nuclear explosion! Today we're either in a war someplace or on the verge of one. Taxes are sapping our economic strength. Crime is going up. The world is in the worst shape it has ever been. Frankly, Dr. Schwartz, I think a man has to be stupid to be optimistic today."

I paused for a moment, then explained that I could understand his viewpoint. (It never does any good to contradict someone. If you want to change their viewpoint, you've got to show understanding first, not argue.)

Then I explained something which I hope got through. I told him this: "You know, sir, there has not been a generation since the dawn of recorded history that didn't believe the world was on the verge of total collapse." I quickly traced some of the frightful worries recorded in the Old Testament, reviewed some of the prophets of gloom and doom in the Roman Empire, and then wound up describing recent generations in our own country.

I showed my pessimistic friend how every generation has the same element—a crowd of negative "fraidy cats" who, perhaps subconsciously, *want* our civilization to go to pot. And whether or not it's subconsciously intentional, this pessimistic talk doesn't solve any problems. It simply muddies up the water and makes it harder for the minority of us who think optimism to make the necessary improvements.

"You know something," I concluded, "our scientists estimate the Earth and our solar system will last roughly 30 *billion* more years.

"And," I told him, "I have an idea man in one form or another is going to be around most of that time."

All of us who want the big, successful happy life must learn to take pessimistic talk in stride.

Get your psyche conditioned. Think, "It's a good world," and it really is!

MAKE THE POINTS IN THIS CHAPTER FOREVER YOURS:

1. Accept the basic success truth, "Thinking Does Make It so."

2. Think, "I Choose to Feel Good," and you do.

3. Think, "I Choose to Be Happy," and you are.

4. Think, "I Choose to Think Rich," and you are.

5. Think, "I Choose to Believe Things Will Get Better," and they do.

6. Think, "It's a Good World," and it is!

Tell your psyche to think the way you want to think.

How To Triple
Your Mental Prowess
And Let Your Brain
Make You Rich

9

How Much Better Must You Be to Be Worth 5 Times as Much?

Here's a question it will pay to ask yourself: Is the person making $50,000 a year 500 percent better than the fellow earning $10,000?

Now, if we define "better" in terms of I.Q. we know immediately that no one is 500 percent smarter than anyone else. Again, if we use "better" to mean skill or physical stamina or effort we know no one has 500 percent edge over anyone else.

What then, explains the enormous difference in the income of people?

I first learned this exciting truth a few years ago. I had just attended a concert by one of America's foremost pianists. After the concert I confessed to my friend, who was my host and knows far more about music than I, "You know, Jim, I couldn't detect too much difference between that fellow and a dozen other pianists I've heard. What's so special?"

Jim then gave me this valuable lesson. "The difference? There isn't much. There are maybe 10,000, maybe even 20,000 piano players who can play 99 percent as well as this fellow. But this pianist has that extra percentage point. He put perhaps 1% more into it and walks off with $1,500 for the concert. His competition lacks that 1%. They get $50 to $100 for playing the same music. The difference between a topnotch pro and a good amateur is often very, very little."

"Are you saying," I suggested, "that you don't have to be 10 times as good to make 10 times as much money?"

"Exactly," my friend agreed. "Take baseball, for example. The fellow who gets a hit 2 times in 10 times at bat is strictly average. In fact he probably won't last the season. But the guy who gets a base hit 3 times in 10—he's the big hero and makes the money."

I've reflected often on this great lesson. The same rule applies across the board. In selling, the fellow who closes one more sale in 10 presentations than the average is going to make money.

The executive who puts 10 percent more into his job often doubles or triples his income. The typical student who studies 10 percent more can easily raise his grade from C— to A.

I have what should be a wonderful surprise for you! Here it is: If you get 10 percent better at whatever you are doing, you should be able to increase your income by 100 percent to 500 percent and more.

The difference between the $7,500 middle management executive and the one earning $15,000 is always less than 10 percent. You may be a physician, lawyer, executive, accountant, salesman, it makes no difference. Just get 10 percent better and you'll at least double your income.

Just try and see!

Ironically, people work hard to get even with the average. But then they stop. With just a fraction more effort they could launch themselves far above the world of mediocrity.

What's the secret to developing that extra 10 percent mental power? Let's start at the beginning.

We've made two outstanding discoveries about mental power. First, long ago at the dawn of civilization, man discovered he could think. Now man stumbled along knowing he had a "thinking machine" for a long time before he knew how to use it properly. He made discoveries by accident. His inventions were accidents. His accomplishments were accidents. Virtually all human progress was accidental.

Then, in relatively recent times, man made the second great discovery. This second discovery is that your brain, your "thinking machine," can be controlled, managed, disciplined; that is, that you can make your mind do what you want it to do, that you can control your mind essentially the same way you control a machine —you can turn it on or you can turn it off. You can adjust its speed of operation within wide limits. You can make it do your bidding. Now, of course, no one has complete control over their thought machine. But with practice, with deliberate attention, far more control can be achieved.

Here are five rules below that show how:

Rule #1. Practice thinking to develop mental thrust. A few years ago I saw an athletic coach working in a health studio. There were about 10 men in his class, most of whom were in pretty flabby shape. They were doing a routine series of calisthenics. And it was pretty obvious that most of the people there were just watching the instructor. He was doing the calisthenics with vigor and was working up quite a sweat. But his students, middle aged men who had paid good money to get back in good physical condition, were taking part in a very half-hearted, unenthusiastic manner.

Finally, the instructor, obviously exasperated, said in his broken English, "Look, youse guys, I've got news for you. You won't build your muscles watching me build mine." He then proceeded to admonish the group that their bodies would not trim up watching the instructor trim his body.

So it is with brains too. The brain needs exercise to do its best work. You've probably heard the story about the school boy who came home, played too hard, and got too tired to do his homework. So he put his books under his pillow hoping the brain by some osmotic process would absorb the lessons he should have studied.

You can't develop your mind just by watching another person develop his mind. You've got to get in there and *practice* thinking if you are going to have first rate creative intelligence.

Thinking is work. To develop our thinking process we must put the mind through exercises which lead it down new paths.

I have a professor acquaintance who has spent almost a lifetime sponging up ideas of other people. His mind is like a library. It's stuffed full of facts. Yet, he is incapable of creative thought because he simply hasn't practiced thinking. If you need facts in this fellow's area, see him. But if you want ideas, if you want progressive suggestions, if you want creative thought, stay away. He simply hasn't developed his creative mental machinery. He is mentally constipated. He can't digest knowledge and come up with new thoughts.

What's behind mental sluggishness? Why is it we are "too soon old and too late smart?" Why do we learn so little after we reach adulthood?

There are many reasons perhaps, but I think the basic one is we grow mentally flabby for essentially the same reason we grow physically flabby. Either we have the wrong kind of diet or we fail to stay in good condition.

Some people have what I like to call "an airconditioned brain" because air is the only thing that seems to penetrate. These people hear noise but never seem to hear thoughts. Now the brain, your psyche, the most magnificent instrument we know of in all the universe, is much too valuable to be used as a noise absorber. The intent, the reason you have a brain, is for you to use it.

It seems to be a natural human tendency to avoid thinking. (As man evolved, thinking was the last thing to develop.) Every evening, many people say in effect, "Here, Mr. TV, absorb my brain." "Here, Mr. Newspaper, occupy my brain for me."

In recent years there has been much concern over the vast increase in spectator sports. Instead of getting out there and playing touch football, most of us go to stadiums and watch the team play. Or instead of playing baseball, we go to the ball park and watch the pros play. Now you and I know that we can watch the 20-game winner pitch Sunday after Sunday and at the end of a season not be able to throw the ball one bit better for all the watching, unless of course, we go home after the game and practice.

Here is one technique to use to develop mental thrust: Deliberately, yes *deliberately,* expose yourself to new problems, and new situations that require you to think.

Let me explain.

Modern military officers are not just sent to school where they can listen to dull lectures. They are told to participate and actually solve real problems.

An engineering company I know, when the work gets slack, keeps its engineers experimenting with brand new designs. Not only is this an excellent way to build brain capital, it's a good device for keeping men interested in their work.

And a father I know asks his children to tell him stories just as often as he tells them a story. "Letting the kids tell me a story develops their brains," he says.

Recently, I heard an insurance executive commenting on what he calls "the sin of sophistication." He illustrated it this way. "Let's say you hire a new secretary. During the first two weeks she learns a lot. She finds out where the restroom is, what the lunch hours are, what time you come to work, how you like your name signed, etc. When you add it all up, she really does learn a lot in two weeks. But then what happens? Then she gets sophisticated and knows her job well enough to virtually coast along not learning anything new.

"Her brain doesn't grow because she stops practicing thinking. She stops looking for new things because she no longer has to."

The same executive, who happens to be executive vice president of his company, said to me, "You know, Dave, I'm so glad that I've been able to switch jobs in my company every three or four years. I'm continually learning something new. I'm continually stimulated as a result of being through so many departments. I now know my company very well."

Remember this: There seems to be little if any correlation between length of time lived and quantity of wisdom absorbed. Often, the only difference between the wisdom quotient of the typical person 18 and the typical person 80 is that the fellow who is 80 is more confused than the person 18.

Follow this rule. Constantly search for new challenges for your thinking process. At work ask for new types of jobs which you really don't know but would like to learn. Seek out the unknown. Tangle with it, conquer it.

Now, here's another way you can develop mental thrust and get an edge over competition. *Go back to school—even if it's only a few hours a month—but go back to school.*

Today, thanks to the big push for more and better education, you can study any one of hundreds of interesting subjects. Education makes you more alert, keeps you young, helps make you interesting to other people and, most important of all, helps you develop mental thrust.

But there is one big danger. Adult education is something everyone is for but relatively few support.

I've observed that when educational programs are offered to the adults, most of the people involved, especially those who need it most, are inclined to find some good rational reason for not taking advantage of the education. Everybody is for it but few people, when given the chance, will accept it.

Another danger is the tendency to take a course and do as little as possible to get by to avoid exercising the brain. People who want to be spoon fed are like the woman who went to the supermarket, purchased a pound of steak, but found only 8 ounces in the pound and then went back to the store to tell the merchant how glad she is to be cheated.

The educational opportunities are there. Why not take advantage? The association with other creative minds in itself is worth many times the cost. I've often been asked by people whether I think night school is good for adults. I often ask them, "Do you go bowling?" If they say "Yes" I'll tell them that one evening a week in some adult program will do them certainly as much good as bowling.

Rule #2. Add width to your thinking. Here's the second basic rule for conditioning your brain to work more effectively for you: Put width into your thinking process.

Narrow-minded people have these characteristics, all negative.

1. They see only a small part of problems.
2. Narrow-minded people are exceptionally prejudiced. They can hate intensely.
3. They are intellectually blind. They learn no wisdom as they mature.

To appraise the width of your thinking, ask yourself this question, "Have I looked at this problem from all sides? Have I thought of a balanced solution?"

HOW WIDE DO YOU THINK?

Situation	Narrow Thinker	Broad Thinker
1. Impression of the President	"The President is stupid. Everything is bungled up."	"Well, I think the President is doing a fine job domestically. I believe certain aspects of our foreign policy could be handled better."

2. Impression of a writer	"I haven't read anything he's written and what's more, I never will. They ought not publish what he writes."	"I haven't formed an opinion of him because I haven't read anything he's written. I hope to soon, however."
3. Immigration policy	"They ought to lock the gate once and for all. All those immigrants do is take jobs that belong to Americans."	"I believe we should have a fair policy—that is, keep the door open but be more selective. We need more good minds in this country and immigration is one way to get them."
4. Non-conformist behavior of a leading movie actress and actor	"Those people are simply awful. They should be locked up. Somebody ought to organize a boycott against their movies."	"It's their life. To each his own. Besides, prominent people deserve privacy. I'm too busy trying to solve my own problems to be concerned with theirs."
5. Living in New York	"They could test an H Bomb there and I wouldn't care. New Yorkers don't give a damn about anybody but themselves. And they are in a hurry to go no-place."	"Living in New York, like living anywhere else, has its pros and cons. No place has all the advantages. But as far as the people are concerned, I think they're as good and as bad as people in any other city."
6. Impression of automobiles	"Those people in Detroit are crazy. They don't know how to design cars. Europe has us beat to pieces in knowing how to design and build cars."	"It depends on what you want to use the automobile for. Now for travel I like the American cars much better. But if I wanted economy, I'd buy a European car. The cars just aren't comparable."

To think wide, remember:

1. Be careful of generalizing with the "all white all black" approach. A quick, impromptu generalization says, "That fellow hasn't considered this. He's talking off the top of his head."

2. Avoid phrases like, "I hate," "They're stupid," and "He's no good."

3. Think two sides before you make your point. Nothing is all good and nothing is all bad.

4. Don't be a "fast gun" with your opinions. In conversation the last man to draw usually wins. Go slow before you take a definite stand on a debatable subject.

Rule #3. Think like a crew member, not like a passenger. In just about every kind of job you find two kinds of people, the passengers and the crew members. Both are on the payroll but the performance of each is different. This difference is in attitude.

The third step in acquiring new mental force is to think like a member of the crew, to project yourself into the situation and assume responsibility for what happens.

Just compare the difference in thinking in these examples.

Passengers	*Crew Members*
1. This isn't my company. What do I care if ...	This is my company. I do care ...
2. Relaxes. "As long as I'm being paid, what difference does it make?"	Digs in. Honestly believes he owes the organization something in return for pay.
3. Looks at the clock as if it were an idol.	Is less concerned about time put in as he is about work turned out.
4. Feels the organization should take care of him.	Feels that he should take care of the organization.

Here's a clue. You can just about always pick out the passengers from the crew by listening to whether they say, "we" or "I," or whether they say, "they."

We find too many passengers in churches, among students, in offices, in the military—just about everywhere.

Be a crew member, not a passenger, *if you plan to arrive.*

There's no easier, more certain way to separate the people who are headed upward from those who are headed nowhere by whether they say "they" or "we."

Examples: The salesman who responds to a question about his company with, "I don't know why 'they' think that way." A management consultant told me recently, "It may seem unimportant, but saying 'they' is like a psychological explosion to the trained ear."

Not long ago I was talking with a young Jaycee. In the course of our conversation I asked him what the Jaycees were doing this year about their highway safety program. To this he replied, "I don't know what 'they' are going to do." Can you visualize this young man becoming president of his Jaycee group?

An executive said, "I feel so strongly on this I require everyone in my organization to say 'we,' never 'they,' in any and all references to the company. I'll fire someone for saying 'they' because anyone who says 'they' isn't, psychologically, working for my company."

Rule #4. Listen—then trade minds with people you want to influence. A few weeks ago I had an opportunity to judge an advertising contest. Radio and television commercials were submitted by various advertising agencies and from these the other judges and I selected the winner. Later I got to chatting with the president of the agency which had won first prize both in the radio and television classifications. I asked him to what he attributed his success—how was he able to develop such powerful commercials.

He looked off in the distance and slowly began to explain. "You know, selling is needed in every human situation. For example, the way a kid gets his dad to buy a $30 baseball glove. That's salesmanship. Or getting people to smoke a certain brand of cigarettes, that's salesmanship. Life itself is one big sale—even getting a woman to marry you, that requires salesmanship."

I interrupted him and rephrased my question. "But what does it take to create an ad that really gets through, one that makes people really want to buy?"

He was ready when I asked that question.

"Well," he said, "I'm lucky. After the war I got out of the service and like most of the fellows, I didn't know anything well. I had never had a real job before I had gone in and I had learned nothing in the service of any benefit to me when I got out. But I differed from most G. I.'s. I had a plan. I was going to go to school. Now, I needed more money than I could get from my G. I. check, so I got a job driving a city bus.

"Well, for five years I drove the bus up and down the streets and went to school at night. Really, I guess I would have been bored silly except this was a good job for it was helping me get through school.

"To conquer the boredom I developed the habit of talking to people, all of them—little old ladies, students, factory workers, mothers with youngsters, all kinds of people. I talked and I got a feel for the way people think. And you know, I think today the reason the advertising we produce is so successful is because I learned to know people." Here he interrupted and asked me this question, "Do you really want to know what's wrong with most advertising?"

I replied that I sure did inasmuch as advertising is one of my principal professional interests.

"Well, it's this," he said. "Too many agencies go out and hire the bright boys fresh out of the Ivy League schools. Now that's all right. We need smart people in the ad business, real smart people. But what most of these young men lack is that they don't really understand people. They study Philosopher Plato and Philosopher Aristotle and that's fine. But, Dave," he said, "they don't study Philosopher Bill Smith, who makes $90 a week and Philosopher Tom Brown, who has his mother-in-law living with him.

"Now I was lucky. I learned what Plato and Aristotle had to say. But where my luck came in, I was able to bridge the philosophy of the great minds and the philosophy of the average man. I learned to know what people think. I learned how to tune in.

"Today," he said, "I can talk to anybody at any level. I was on a committee not long ago that visited the President. I had no trouble talking to him, but I can also talk to the indigent worker, the out-of-work individual, the little people, big people, middle-size people.

"So, my first rule for a successful business has been to listen. Listen, and *feel* along with them. I'm not telling them my views. I'm asking them for theirs. You see the trouble is most of us, when we talk to people, really aren't listening. We're like two kids coming back from Christmas holidays. The first kid asks the second, 'What did you do over the holidays?' So the second begins to tell. But the first kid isn't listening, he's just watching until the second kid comes up for air, and then he is going to tell what he did. Well, this is the way most so-called conversation takes place. I learned to listen to people driving that bus. I didn't argue with them. I didn't tell them I think they are wrong. I would probe and probe trying to find out more about what they thought and why they thought that way.

"You'd be amazed how many fellows who try to write advertising directed at farmers haven't talked to a real for-sure farmer in ten years, possibly never. We've got people trying to influence truck drivers or bricklayers who've never talked to or been in a truck stop or a union hiring hall. Don't try to determine if the other fellow is right or wrong. Just try to figure him out."

Isn't this a wonderful communication lesson?

I know a fellow who was preparing a speech on the social impact of unemployment. He went to the library, dug out the latest journals, business magazines, collected a huge stack of statistics and gave his speech. It was not very well received. It was just another speech.

A second fellow, having the same assignment, instead of seeing how many statistics he could collect, went out and actually talked to unemployed people. He asked them what they were doing, how they were getting by, what they thought about, what their politics were—he asked them all of these many, many pressing questions.

Guess whose speech went over best.

Remember Rule #4, listen, then trade minds with people you want to influence.

School teachers can teach school better if they visit some of the homes of the children. Preachers can preach better if they visit the homes and talk to the people in their usual circumstances.

Remember, it isn't how much you talk. It's how much you listen that determines if your brain will develop understanding and power to convince other people.

Take this test for yourself to see if your brain is getting maximum exposure. Ask yourself:

How long has it been since you have carried on a one-minute conversation with a farmer? A school teacher? A bricklayer? A gangster? A convicted criminal? A senior executive? The janitor who cleans up long after you have gone? A garbage man? A professor? A minister?

It's a hard test, but it's one we all need to take. If we are to make our living influencing people, doesn't it make sense to listen and trade brains with the people we're trying to sell?

Rule #5. Develop your own "wisdom builder." On a recent visit to Minneapolis a lawyer friend, who was my host, invited me to dinner. After dinner we went into his private study and he told me, "I've got something I want to show you." It was what he called a "wisdom builder."

Needless to say I was quite fascinated because I had never heard of a "wisdom builder" before. So I naturally asked, "What is it? How does it work?"

His "wisdom builder" looked on the surface very much like a large diary. He explained it worked this way, "Each evening I review my experiences of that day. Then I try to draw a message

7

from the day s events. Next I wrote down in a sentence or two a summary of the principle involved. Let me show you a few." There was one that said, "Avoid appearing to know too much. Never try to show off your .brain power." He explained that he had put that one down one day because he had had an experience in which he lost a lot of legal ground because he acted as if he were too sharp. He made the judge feel foolish and the judge later penalized him.

Another bit of wisdom that he showed me read, "Plan tomorrow's activities today. You'll have time and use your brain more effectively." Others dealt with a wide range of matters—why it's foolish to argue, tell people they are wrong, and so on.

I was quite impressed with this, for it looked like an excellent documentation of practical wisdom.

"How did you happen to develop this habit?" I asked.

"Well," he explained, "I've always been interested in self-betterment. But the real thing that got me started was back in college. I had to do a term project on the life of Benjamin Franklin. Well, as I got to studying I learned something that I didn't know about Benjamin Franklin's rules for success. I learned that he wrote *Poor Richard's Almanac* for himself as a guide to his own behavior. He didn't write these rules for publication, although later friends urged him to print his practical philosophy and thus share it with the world.

"Well, it made sense to me that if Benjamin Franklin could write some advice to himself every day, I guess I could too. If it worked for him, it should work for me. So, I began this habit and now I never fail to go to bed at night without trying to draw one rule from the lessons of the day just ended. I carry this wisdom builder with me on trips and often pull it out of my brief case when I'm on an airplane.

"Of course, there is nothing original here. You could find the same rules for successful living in a dozen books. But it means so much more to me because I discovered these on my own. This is not second-hand wisdom."

Isn't that a wonderful idea? My friend went on to tell me

how he credits this with helping him avoid making the same mistake too many times. "I learned something else back there in school. It goes like this, 'Fool me once, shame on you. Fool me twice, shame on me.'"

I'm sure you know a number of people who keep diaries. And I'll bet most of these folks will put down comments such as this one which is typical: "Today was another gloomy day. It rained. Martha called to say she was sick. Tomorrow I'll go to the Doctor."

But my lawyer friend is different—and smarter too. He concluded this part of our conversation with a comment I'll always remember.

"You know, some people keep a diary of all the terrible things that happen to them every day. I don't. All I want to do is keep the distilled essence of life. I am striving to develop wisdom."

Many great men use this wisdom building device. David, one of the principal contributors to the Bible and one of history's truly profound thinkers, wrote Proverbs to guide and understand himself. David did not sit down and say to himself, "Today, I'm going to write another chapter in the Bible to tell other people how they ought to live." Rather, David wrote Proverbs to give direction to himself. And as a natural by-product of putting down the lessons he learned, David increased his leadership ability.

We can be sure of this: while hundreds of millions of people have studied the ageless wisdom of David, the one person who benefited most was David himself. It helped make him a creative psychologist and a master philosopher.

Will this wisdom building technique help you? I believe it will. Here's all you need do. First, get yourself a diary or notebook. Second, each day write the answer to this question in your diary, *"What great lesson did I learn today?"* Third, keep this up without missing a day for one month. Then spend a couple hours reviewing all the "wisdoms" you've jotted down. Then, if you find it pays, as I'm sure you will, just keep it up.

Here's why this program works. The raw material of wisdom (practical philosophy and applied psychology) is all around you, in the many incidents, big and little, which make up every-day life. And the process of writing these lessons down constitutes organized soul searching. Remember too, when you write, your mental energy, 100 percent of it, is concentrated on thinking. What you write, you will remember 10 times as clearly as what you speak. Pencil and paper—these are the powerful tools of wisdom building. Use them.

Use "Wisdom Building" at Work, Too

We can use the wisdom building technique just described in our work too. The wisdom of successful business is found in situations all around us. Let me give you another example.

A few months ago, a former student of mine, in business for just four years, opened his fourth hardware store. This was quite a feat, considering the young fellow's small initial capital investment of only $3,500, strong competition from other stores, and the relatively short time he had been in business.

I visited his new store shortly after it opened to congratulate him on the fine progress he had made. In an indirect way I asked him how he was able to make a success of three stores and open a fourth one when most merchants had to struggle to make a success of just one store.

"Naturally," he answered, "I worked hard, but just getting up early and working late isn't responsible for the four stores. Most people in my business work hard. The main thing I attribute my success to is my self-styled 'weekly improvement program.'"

"A weekly improvement program? Sounds impressive. How does it work?" I asked.

"Well, it really isn't anything elaborate," he continued. "It's just a plan to help me to do a better job as each week rolls around.

"To keep my forward thinking on the track, I've divided my job into four elements: customer, employees, merchandise, and promotion. All during the week I make notes and jot down ideas as to how I can improve my business. Then every Monday evening I set aside three hours to review the ideas I've jotted down and figure out how to put the solid ones to use in the business." (He pulled a notebook from his pocket to show me.) "In this three-hour period I force myself to take a hard look at my operation. I don't simply wish more customers would shop in my store. Instead I ask myself, 'What can I do to attract more customers? How can I develop regular, loyal customers?' "

He went on describing numerous little innovations that made his first three stores so successful—things like the way he arranged the merchandise within his stores, his suggestion-selling technique that sold two out of three customers merchandise they had not planned to buy when they entered his stores, the credit plan he devised when many of his customers were out of work because of a strike, the contest he developed that boosted sales during a slack season.

"I ask myself," he went on, " 'what can I do to improve my merchandise offerings?' and I get ideas. Let me cite just one case. Four weeks ago it occurred to me that I should do something to get more youngsters into the store. I reasoned if I had something here to draw the kids to the store I'd also draw more of the parents. I kept thinking about it and then this idea came: Put in a line of small carded toys for children in the four-to-eight age bracket. It's working. The toys take little space and I make a nice profit on them. But most important, the toys have increased store traffic.

"Believe me," he went on, "my weekly improvement plan works. Just by conscientiously asking myself, 'How can I do a better job?' I find the answers. It's a rare Monday night that I don't come up with some plan or technique that makes profit and loss statements look better. And I've learned something else too about successful merchandising, something that I think every person going into business for himself should know."

"What's that?" I asked.

"Just this. It isn't so much what you know when you start that matters. It's what you learn and put to use after you open your doors that counts most."

Big success calls for persons who continually set higher standards for themselves and others, persons who are searching for ways to increase efficiency, to get more output at lower cost, do more with less effort. Top success is reserved for the I-can-do-it-better kind of person.

General Electric uses the slogan: Progress is our most important product.

Why not make progress your most important product?

The I-can-do-better philosophy works magic. When you ask yourself, "How can I do better?" your creative power is switched on and ways for doing things better suggest themselves.

Here is a daily exercise that will help you discover and develop the power of the I can-do-better attitude. Each day before you begin work, devote ten minutes to thinking "How can I do a better job today?" Ask, "What can I do today to encourage my employees?" "What special favor can I do for my customers?" "How can I increase my personal efficiency?"

This exercise is simple. But it works. Try it and you'll find unlimited creative ways to win greater success.

POINTS TO REMEMBER IN THIS CHAPTER

1. Remember, you don't have to be 500 percent better to earn 500 percent more money. Usually, the difference is very, very small between top notch producers and the multitudes of mediocre people. Big achievement comes from controlled thinking.

2. Use your mind—practice thinking to develop mental power. Put yourself through some vigorous mental exercises every day. Don't fall into the trap of believing you can build your mental muscles by watching other people develop theirs.

3. Get the big view. Put width into your thinking. Train yourself to see the whole picture—not just a piece of it.

4. Think like a crew member not like a passenger. Think "I" and "we." Never think "they." "They" thinkers are destined to remain second raters.

5. *Practice the trade minds technique. Listen to the people you want to influence. Don't relax until you can speak with and understand people in every walk of life and on every socio-economic level.*

6. *Develop your own wisdom builder. Keep notes on lessons you've learned. Remember, when you write them down you write permanent instructions to your mental computer.*

How To Consolidate Your Psychic
Power And Increase Its
Benefits Every Year
Of Your Life

10

All of us have heard this quotation many times: "The saddest words of tongue or pen are these, *it might have been*." Let me tell you about an incident that illustrates just how sad the words "it might have been" really are. Last June I spoke at the annual convention for a large company. At this convention one of the old-timers was singled out for retirement. The president of the company got up, made the usual routine remarks about "how valuable Harry had been" and " how we all would miss him."

After my talk I chatted with the well-wishers and then started to leave. But Harry, the retiree who had been almost ignored after the ceremonies, tapped me on my arm and asked, "Have you got 30 minutes? I've got to talk to somebody."

How could I refuse a request like that? So I said, "Of course," and we went to my suite, ordered some sandwiches and got comfortable. It was easy to see Harry was discouraged.

I opened things up by saying, "Well, this is sure a big night for you, retiring after all these years. I'm so glad you wanted to talk with me." (I knew Harry was uncomfortable and I wanted to make it easy for him to talk.)

"That's just it," Harry opened up. "I'm not happy. This is one of the saddest nights of my life."

"Why?" I asked, trying to imply I was surprised when in truth I wasn't.

"Well, tonight I just sat there and came face-to-face with a wasted life. It sounded good, I know," Harry explained, "but the truth is I feel like I'm a complete failure."

"What are you going to do now?" I asked, "you're only 65." (I wanted to get him thinking forward instead of backward.)

"What do you think," he said sharply, indicating disgust with himself. "I'm going to continue living scared right down to the very end. My wife and I are going to move down to Old Folksville, Florida, and sit there until I die. I've got a little pension and social security which will put me in one of those little houses where I can finish dying.

"And you know," he added bitterly, "I hope it comes quick." There was a moment of silence and then he took his watch from his pocket—it was still in the case—and said, "I think I'll give this away. I don't want to be reminded."

"Do you want to tell me about it?" I asked.

Harry was a little more relaxed now and he went on. "You can't imagine how hurt I was tonight when George (the President of the company) got up to give his little speech. George and I joined the company together. But George pushed ahead. And I didn't. The most I ever made with the company was $7,250 a year. Last I heard George was making 10 times that, not counting all the bonuses and other benefits. As I look back at it, George wasn't any smarter. He just wasn't scared. He jumped in. I didn't.

"It wasn't that opportunity never knocked. It did. Lots of times both in the company and out. After I'd been in the company five years I had a chance to go South and manage the Southern Division. But I turned it down because I felt I couldn't handle it.

There were other times too, but every time my chance came, I found an excuse for backing off.

"Now, it's all over and I've got nothing but disappointments to remember my life. As I sit it out down there in Old Folksville, I'll have nothing but time to reflect on my wasted life.

"Oh I got by all right, a fair middle-class life. We ate well enough, my wife never had expensive clothes but she dressed okay. We took a few vacations. And I helped the kids go to college.

"Right there," Harry broke in, having touched a particularly sensitive spot, "is where it really hurts. I have two sons and I think they've sensed since they were youngsters that I'm basically a coward."

Harry talked on and on. Over and over in many different ways he explained his intense dissatisfaction with the way he had failed to stand up and live.

It all added up to proving the enormous insight in that eternal wisdom: "The saddest words of tongue or pen are these, it might have been."

Harry had drifted, with no real goal. Harry had been afraid to live, afraid to step out and assume responsibility. Harry had lived only to "get by." And now, at the end of his career, he could look back and stare at a wasted life. Harry, like millions of people, many of whom you know, had sentenced himself to a lifetime of psychological slavery.

If you aren't doing what you'd like to do; if you're holding yourself back; if you aren't getting excitement from life; if you just plain aren't living; then read very closely what follows. I'm going to describe for you a six-point program that shows you how to *consolidate all of your psychic power* so you can multiply your success in any field you choose.

Just as a small insignificant-looking child's magnifying glass can, when manipulated properly, concentrate so much of the sun's rays as to cause a fire, so you, with your psychic power consolidated, can multiply your income and happiness, and put yourself in the kind of psychological orbit you really want.

This psychic consolidation program involves these specific steps:

1. Divorce yourself from psychological slavery.

2. Cure yourself of all forms of goal alibitis.

3. Draw up your "will for living."

4. Realize you already have the raw material of which money is made.

5. Then, discover the fact that money is enormously plentiful and you can have any amount you really want.

6. Understudy only the most successful people.

Let's get going with Step #1 as follows:

Divorce yourself from slavery. Some years ago I arranged for a group of students to visit a large factory. Some of them, as you would expect, had not been inside a factory before. About midway through the plant the tour was interrupted and the group and I spent a few minutes in an employee cafeteria drinking coffee. I asked the students at my table for their impressions of what they had seen so far.

One student spoke up and with a perplexed look he said, "Well, I don't know what to think. I'm very depressed. So many of those people out there look like slaves. Few of them look like they like their work. Frankly they seem to hate their jobs." Others in the group chipped in. They had received the same general reaction.

As we continued our tour, the remark, "So many of those people out there look like slaves," dominated my thinking. The student was right, perhaps more right than he knew.

At one machine I observed a woman employee who had the I-don't-like-this-job-but-I-have-to-eat-so-I've-resigned-myself-to-it look. I wondered as I watched her why she was here at this particular job while many of her feminine counterparts were doing exciting things. Perhaps this woman could be in another career? Perhaps entertaining some friends this afternoon? Perhaps she could be smiling rather than looking like she hated everyone and everything. Perhaps she could be doing any one of many wonderful things. But she was here—in slavery.

At another machine I watched a fellow, about 50 or so, explain what he was doing and how he did it. He appeared to know his job thoroughly. And he seemed quite intelligent. But it was equally obvious that he was there because he "had to be." He too was a slave. Could he have been doing something else? Could he have been an engineer? Perhaps with the proper training he could have designed equipment to completely automate the work done by persons in his operation.

Other people there might have been chemists, writers, merchants, executives, salesmen. But to use the words of my student, they were slaves.

We do have much slavery in the 20th century. And slavery is not confined to any kind of work. There are slaves in offices, stores, on farms, and everywhere else.

Note this: Modern-day slaves are slaves by their own personal choice, not because someone forced them into slavery. They unwittingly choose slavery because they don't know how to be free.

Modern-day slavery is mental, not physical. Today's slave has his mind, his ambition, his desire controlled by someone else. True he is not *physically* in chains and he is not *physically* beaten. But today's slave is very much in a mental prison where he suffers tremendous psychological punishment in the form of doing work he hates, letting others control his future, and knowing while this is going on that he *could* and *should* be enjoying life.

Success requires freedom. And freedom in this case comes from surrender—surrender to the one biggest, most challenging thing you want to do and you'll find freedom and success.

Be free! Refuse to be a 20th century slave. Many people are dissatisfied, gloomy, and failing for this simple reason. They have failed to select a target toward which they can enthusiastically concentrate all their energies. Most people who are standing still in life aren't going any place for a very simple reason. They haven't selected a place to go. They are just spending themselves, their energy, their talent, aiming at nothing. And when you aim at nothing, you hit nothing.

Take some time right now to ponder one question. It may be the most important question you ever asked yourself. "Who is running your life?" Other people? Your job? I mentioned this just to underscore one point. Life at best is closely rationed. Few people exceed 25,000 days of it. Even with today's medical science, you won't have much more than this.

Step #2. Cure yourself of goal alibitis. Here is an interesting observation. The millions of people who are unhappy in their work—who dislike life, grouch, complain and live in misery—once had a dream of what they wanted. But they didn't follow through. Why? Because they suffer from "goal alibitis."

There are several main types of "goal alibitis." Read them. Then tomorrow start listening to people grumble. Listen, and you'll hear them try to explain away their failures by one of these alibis.

First Alibi: "I've been trained for this profession. I can't afford to waste my training."

CASE OF AN ADVERTISING EXECUTIVE WHO BECAME A RANCHER

M. B. was 43 and an account executive for a major advertising agency when he made a thorough re-appraisal of his career objectives. He explained to me that, while he liked advertising and had devoted twenty years to it, it somehow disagreed with his psychological make-up.

"I know I was doing a fine job," he went on. "I was very well paid. But I was having to drive myself to produce. My doctor explained to me that I was 'working against my will,' which he said was one of the chief ways to damage the heart, stomach, and other vital organs.

"For years I had known what I really wanted to do but I had never told anyone. Working for another agency some time back I was in charge of a feed manufacturer's advertising. I got to know a lot about raising cattle and the more I learned about it, the better I liked it.

"But I felt like a fool every time I thought about giving up advertising. I had gone to college six years to prepare myself for this career. I figured only an idiot would throw away $35,000 worth of education and twenty years' experience.

"Then too, I had another big problem in striking out in a totally different occupation—I have a wife and a teenage daughter. For a long time I was ashamed to even mention what I'd like to do. I could just see my wife laughing at me—and then getting angry—when she knew I 'was on the level' about wanting to give up a good income to go raise cows in South Alabama.

"But one day I mustered the nerve and explained my idea to her. I was sure she'd put the clamps on it. But she didn't! She asked me dozens of questions about the idea. We talked for hours. Finally, after she knew all about my plan, she said, 'I'm with you. When do we start?'

"Later that evening I thanked her intimately and tenderly for having approved the idea. It was then she said one of the finest things any wife ever told her husband. She said, 'I married you. Not your job or your bank account. When you explained ranching to me this afternoon I saw my man full of life and spirit, like I hadn't seen him in years. That is what really counts.'"

M. B. became a rancher. I got a note from him a few months ago. Here's all it said, "Dave, I was a good ad-man, but I'm a terrific rancher. Come to see us."

M. B. is one of a relatively few individuals who proved a person can conquer goal alibitis if he honestly tries!

In the course of a year I meet hundreds of professional people who are very unhappy in their work but stay with it because "I was trained for it." I personally know hundreds of engineers who would be happier (and much richer!) if they were in selling. I know professors who should be in business and businessmen who should be professors. It is amazing when you think of it how few people are really doing the work they enjoy (and then they wonder why they aren't making big money!)

Can I Make It on My Own? Closely related to the "I've-been-trained-for-this-profession-so-I-can't-give-it-up" alibi is the "Can I Make It On My Own?" fear.

Let me tell you about a situation a friend of mine named Andy conquered. Here is what he told me.

"You know, that question 'Can I Make It On My Own?' bothered me for years. I had been with the same company, a department store, for thirteen years. Now, I had originally been trained as an engineer, and I was using my training on the job. But I just didn't like the work.

"I wanted to change jobs but didn't have the nerve. After all, I was over 40 years of age. I had read all the articles about how difficult it is to relocate once you've passed 40. My wife had read the articles too, and she was naturally scared. How would we keep up the mortgage payments? How will we send our teenage children to college?

"I've been struggling like this for three or four years. But I just couldn't get going. Every day I dragged myself to my job in the store. I did it reasonably well, at least well enough to get by. Then at night I'd go home to become even more frustrated. I even started to drink more than was good for me.

"Then something happened, almost like an answer to prayer. In fact later, as I think about it, I believe it truly was an answer to prayer even though I didn't consciously know that I had been praying for it."

"What was it?" I asked, half-way expecting to hear him say that he had inherited a million dollars.

"Just this," he answered, "I was fired. Out of a clear blue sky I was called into the president's office, given a severance check and let go.

"I was stunned for a while, but after a couple of days I began to see that this was really good. My wife wanted to know who I was going to work for now. I was proud to tell her, 'Myself.'

"As I look back at it," my friend went on, "I had been like a fully grown bird that's afraid to fly. I had to be pushed out of my nest to get going and that's what being fired did for me."

Andy went on to tell me how he put down on paper what he could do, what he would like to do, what he thought he could offer in business for himself. He established himself as a technical consultant in traffic management. This meant he would go to a company and show them how they could handle their delivery problems with fewer personnel and less cost.

It's been three years since Andy was fired. What has been the result? Andy is now making over $40,000 a year which is exactly two and a half times what he had been making in his job. In other words, he gained 250 percent in income in less than three years.

But the money is really not what is important here. The key thing is that Andy is again *alive*. His old complaints about his back and about his headaches, and about being tired plus all the inner frustration are gone.

I sometimes wonder what would happen to the health of this country if all of us would do the jobs we really wanted to do. I think we would just about put the pill makers out of business. It seems all of the modern day excesses, excessive smoking, excessive drinking, excessive headaching, excessive pill taking, excessive speeding, all of these and many more excessives are traced back to a form of psychological slavery.

Every day an estimated 40,000 people are fired. And in at least 95 percent of these cases, these people should be grateful that they've been pushed out of the nest so they have a chance to really fly.

Second Alibi: "I'm too old to start over."

This alibi is terribly common, and contrary to popular opinion, it isn't restricted to people over 40 or 50. I know many young people in their twenties and thirties who are "too old" to give up a career they don't like.

Let me give you the case history of Miss J.H.P., who was an elementary school teacher for 25 years. She liked her work because she knew it was important and she loved young children. But she confessed teaching in public schools was not her chief ambition.

"Long ago, way back when I was in college," she explained, "I pictured myself operating my own kindergarten. One of my

professors made a big point of explaining to us that thought patterns of children are surprisingly fixed before they reach school
age. I saw that working with pre-school age children would be a
lot of fun. And besides, if I had my own kindergarten I'd have
much more freedom.

"But my trouble was I just dreamed and that's all. Every
time I came near resigning and starting my own kindergarten, I
got panicky. I thought I was too old to give up teaching. And I
could just see my modest savings lost.

"Well, I kept waiting another 'year or two,' but every year
making the change seemed more difficult. Finally, when I reached
47, I decided it's now or never. I resigned my job in the spring
and spent the next summer getting my 'pre-school' set up. I used
my savings to make a down payment on an old but large and well-
constructed house. Then I had the first floor remodeled for the
kindergarten and I fixed up the upstairs for my living quarters.
Then, in August, I prepared a simple announcement of my 'pre-
school' and what it was created to do and mailed it to the parents
in the community.

"I've been operating my kindergarten now for four years and
it's a success in every way. I've never been so happy and my
income is over twice what it was when I was in the public schools.
I've got enthusiasm now that I never experienced before."

Miss J.H.P. got rewards—enjoyment, enthusiasm, and sub-
stantially increased income—simply by surrendering to her real
goal.

But note: To get herself going forward, Miss J.H.P. had to
overcome "I'm too old" alibitis.

Third Alibi: "I don't like this job but it's what my parents
wanted."

P.M. is an example of a young man who resisted doing what
he wanted to do because of his parents' wishes, even though his
parents had passed away 13 years ago!

"My father was a small town minister in the mid-west," P.M.
explained to me. "He was a wonderful man. Very good in every

way. I admired and worshipped him. Father had only one wish for me—that I become a minister too. Well, father and mother both died in an accident when I was 14. I spent the next four years with an aunt and uncle. Then I enrolled in a theological school.

"Even then something inside me seemed to tell me that this profession wasn't quite right for me. But when I felt that way I would remind myself that this is what my father wanted me to do and so it was what I must do. After I finished school I tried hard to find challenge and enjoyment in my work but for me, it just wasn't there.

"Two years ago I finally had the courage and wisdom to face up to my situation and where it was leading me. I finally discovered, after much thinking, that I was being unfair to everyone concerned by being something I couldn't put all of myself into. I was being unfair to my congregation for I wasn't as good a minister as they deserved. I was being unfair to my wife and two children too. Even though I concealed my dissatisfaction, it was certain to show through and warp their lives. And I even discovered that I was being grossly unfair to the memory of my father. He wanted me to be a minister, that's true, but I feel my father would have been the first to say, 'Son, do what you feel is really best for you and your family.'

"So, I resigned my pastorate and became a high school music teacher, something I've always wanted to be."

Excessive parental influence is a major factor in many career disappointments. Fathers especially are often very eager to see their sons follow in their footsteps. Adding the words "and Son" to the business or professional name is one of the greatest joys many men look forward to. But two disappointing things often happen when a father pressures a son into joining the family business or following his father's occupation against the son's will. First, the son may refuse, thereby hurting the feelings of the parent. Or, if the son accepts, even though he has no absorbing interest in the activity, he is doomed to mediocre, unhappy performance.

Let me relate one case which illustrates how a young man succeeded after years of disappointment in switching careers to his—and his father's—complete satisfaction.

G. T. lost his left arm to an enemy grenade in World War II. After almost two years in service hospitals, he came home to find that his dad had created a big place for him in the family's industrial equipment supply business. But G. T., then 28, was far from interested.

"I hate to read blueprints. I dislike talking about equipment," G. T. told me at one of our first meetings. And the dissatisfaction grew. It was clear not only from G. T.'s attitude but from psychological and vocational tests as well that G. T. simply was not cut out for the industrial equipment supply business.

Now, what to do? G. T. explained that what he wanted to do most was start an insurance agency. He had become a close friend of another war-caused amputee and the two of them wanted to go into business together. But the hitch was G. T.'s father. G. T. explained that his father had worked hard for many years to build up the business. "Now, if I walk out on him, it will be the greatest disappointment he has ever received."

Over a period of several months we worked out a plan to sell G. T.'s father on the idea that G. T. preferred another type of work.

Here is what G. T. did. He looked at the problem from his father's standpoint a long time. Then he explained to his father that he wanted to do the same thing as the father—achieve success on his own merit. His father understood and G. T. is quite happy and prosperous teamed up with his friend operating an insurance agency.

As a parent it's well to remember that the parent's function is to encourage the child in the child's interests, not his own unless, of course, they are the same.

Often the parental influence is not overtly expressed. Instead it is just felt. The normal child wants to please his parents more than anyone else. The solution then is not found in direct contradiction of the parent's desires. Rather, it requires gaining the parent's appreciation that it is to *his* benefit as well as your own to go the way you really want to go.

Remember these two things about the third alibi, "I don't like this but it's what my parents want."

1. Most of all, your parents want you to *succeed* and *be happy.* Once they understand it's in your interest to do some other type work, they'll be behind you.

2. As a parent, remember how terribly wrong it is psychologically to try and remake your children in your own image.

Fourth Alibi: "I've Got a Good Job Now. I'd Be a Fool to Give It Up."

This is possibly the most common form of goal alibitis you face. People who suffer from this alibi are the type who still believe "A bird in the hand is worth two in the bush."

Such people think, "following the line of least resistance leads to peace of mind."

But they're wrong.

Unfortunately for them, most people ignore that directional signal inside them that points the way to satisfaction and reward. K. D. is one of those. K. D. grew up on a farm in Wisconsin and joined the army shortly after World War II. He's a very intelligent, hard working fellow, and despite no college training he received a peacetime commission in the regular army. While stationed near a large city K. D. because interested in stocks and bonds—so interested that he became a registered representative and started selling mutual funds in his free time.

Over a period of 18 months K. D. became fascinated with securities. And with little effort his commissions from part-time selling soon exceeded his captain's pay. Even more important, K. D. found the field of finance far more interesting than his military career.

The investment company was so impressed with K. D.'s work that they asked him to join them in a management capacity. But K. D. said no. His reasoning was that in ten years he could retire from the army with a pension for life. The pension was just too important to give up. Shortly afterward, K. D. was sent to an overseas base.

Now no one will ever know the wisdom of K. D.'s decision. But several things seem likely. He is trading ten vigorous, profitable years doing what he really wants to do for ten years of doing what is to him relatively unpleasant.

The lives of countless people who face decisions like K. D. show that ignoring the directional signal takes away zest, vigor, and that freshness which spells life.

"I'm too near retirement," "I've put in too many years in this company," are common forms of goal alibitis.

Often a bird in the hand is *not* worth two in the bush.

Have You Made Your Will—Life Will, That Is?

Here is a question I often ask audiences. It helps me make a very special point. "How many of you," I ask, "have written out a plan for dying? Please raise your hands."

People look a little perplexed for a few seconds indicating they don't quite understand what I mean.

Then someone will always say, "Do you mean a will?" And I'll respond with, "Yes, a will or a written plan for dying."

Now, when the "written plan for dying" is interpreted to mean a will, 50 to 75 percent of the hands go up.

"That's fine," I say. "I'm glad to see so many people prepared for death.

"Now," I continue, "how many of you have a written plan for *living*—a plan that spells out where you're going and how you're going to get there?"

If the auditorium is quite large, perhaps two or three hands go up! More than half the people I talk to have written clearly defined plans for death. But not one percent have written, clearly defined plans for life!

A plan for death but no plan for life!

Now, I don't aim to deprecate the importance of a will. It is important and necessary. But honestly now, is a blueprint for dying as important as a blueprint for living? After all, you aren't here when you're dead but you are here when you're alive.

I have been stressing the values of written life plans now for over a decade and I'm beginning to see some positive results. People whom I urged to set up goals years ago are beginning to report back with amazing results.

The case of a goal I described in *The Magic of Thinking Big* has gained far more already than that individual set out to win.

Now we're coming close to the success secret that holds the key to great accomplishment and great reward. *Successful people are those who are doing what they really want to do and are doing it on purpose with a maximum effort.*

Next we come to the most critical step of all. Here it is: Define your purpose. *Define what you really want to do.*

A leading evangelist says his purpose is to "save souls"—not fill churches, not raise lots of money, not build new churches. These things *come automatically* because he is focusing his attention on what is really important.

A successful executive says his purpose is "build this company." Building new plants, setting up new sales agencies, hiring good people—all of these things fall in place because he has his purpose in proper perspective.

Here are others.

A leading politician says—"win votes."
A leading architect says—"create great structures."
Successful car salesman says—"sell cars."
A famous football coach says—"win games."
A successful mother says—"raise children."
A student that's going places says—"develop my mind."
A successful author says—"write books."

And when you've got your purpose analysis burned into your subconscious, then you don't have to worry about how to get where you want to go. A salesman whose objective is "sell cars" is not going to spend too much time drinking coffee or reading magazines. He's going to sell cars!

One danger here is your purpose can be too vague, too confused. You should be able to reduce to no more than three words what your big objective in life is. If it takes more than three words, your goal is still too confused.

Below are several examples to illustrate the right way to define your purpose.

"But I want to make money; where is it?"

Just the other day a 27-year-old man four years out of college came by to see me about additional education. "You see," he began, "I want to study law. But before I take up law I want to know what type law I should practice. I want to go into that branch where the most money is to be made.

"I suppose," he added, "I should study corporation law because I've heard that corporation lawyers make more money than other types of lawyers."

I had a hard time straightening this fellow out. It was difficult to get him to see that every branch of law—criminal, corporation, civil, estate—has plenty of big money opportunities.

"But you've got to be good at it," I explained. "And you can't get really good, really sharp in any field unless you like it," I added. Exceptional people can make money in every field. Or stated another way, every occupation is an acre of diamonds.

So often I meet someone who says something like, "I'm going to get an automobile dealership. There's lots of money in it," or "I'm thinking of getting into insurance. I hear you can make a lot of money," or "I might go into such and such a business. I hear there's a lot of money to be made."

Right here is where most people make an expensive mistake. It's in choosing an occupation where we "hear" there's a "lot of money" being made.

In truth, we do find some car dealers who are rich. But we also find a lot of car dealers going broke and a lot of poor insurance men. Lawyers who barely get by are certainly not rare. Nor are doctors, salesmen, or any other occupational group.

The point is this: every occupation you can think of has its high earners and its very low money makers. Even in the so-called poor pay areas such as teaching and the ministry, I personally know people earning in excess of $50,000 annually. Farming pays poorly, so they say. But I know many rich farmers.

It is infinitely more difficult to determine where the money is NOT, than where the money IS.

In truth, there are no "poor pay" occupations. There are just a lot of people in all occupations who really don't want to be there, have no business being there—people who should get out and take up work they like.

Just recently I heard a story—I checked it out and it is true—about a chemical salesman in New York who was doing only a mediocre job because he simply didn't like his work. He had two chief hobbies—he liked dogs and he liked to walk. So, this enterprising fellow set up a dog walking service for rich New Yorkers and is making upwards of $500 a week *doing what he really likes to do.*

All occupations have a big money promise if you (a) really like it, and (b) give it the maximum effort.

To decide, "I'm going to do such and such because there is money in it," can well be the most stupid decision you will ever make.

To decide, "I'm going to do such and such because it's what I really want to do," is the wisest decision you will ever make.

Promise of money alone is not enough. The work must *appeal* to you; it must attract you, pull you. If it does that, you are virtually certain to make money.

The truth is there is no one best occupation for success. There are no dead-end jobs in America. There are only a lot of dead-end or no-end people. There are barrels of gold in every occupation. And there are barrels of happiness and deep satisfaction too.

"Should I Try to Make Lots of Money?"

Quite a few people today have an odd sort of guilt feeling about wanting to make money. For some reason they want to apologize for having a money goal and are quick to say, "I don't want to be rich—all I want is to make a 'good' living."

Now, let's get one thing straight. Money is not bad. Money, which is the only wholly negotiable form of reward, represents two things: First, money indicates how much socially acceptable service you have given your fellow man. Second, money represents your capacity to do good. A person making $50,000 a year, for example, has twice the capacity to do good as does a person earning $25,000.

A strong desire to accumulate money is healthy, not harmful. And going back to something I've underscored many times in this book, financial independence is a key part in anyone's drive to attain psychic freedom. The people who have licked the money problem are much better positioned to tackle other problems.

The Magic Lesson For Making More Money

Not long ago the president of a bank I know well and I were chatting about what it takes to succeed. My friend asked me a very penetrating question.

"Dave," he said, "do you have any disappointments in your teaching and lecturing efforts? Do you feel people in general fail to grasp any key elements of your wonderful success philosophy?"

I didn't have to think long to answer that question for I do have one big disappointment. That's my inability to get everyone to understand what I call the magic lesson for making money. This lesson, when learned, automatically starts producing more money.

In a nutshell, *the magic lesson for making money is not to make money your primary goal.* This sounds odd, I know, coming from someone who thinks money is good, not evil. Money, to be made in large quantities, must be a secondary goal, not the primary goal.

Let me explain.

I have a good friend, a tree farmer in Middle Georgia. His net worth today is in excess of $2,000,000. And he started from scratch only 16 years ago. He told me recently, "You know, I started out in the late 1940's to become the world's best tree farmer. I love trees. I get enormous fun out of taking old worn-out land and converting it into forests full of young healthy pines.

"Now, I've made a lot of money already and I stand to make a whole lot more. But the funny thing is, I have never been real eager to make money. Somehow, I've just concentrated on growing trees in the very best way possible and money has taken care of itself."

There you have it.

Put money first, and you'll probably stay poor.

Put your *purpose* first, and you're headed toward riches.

Examples of the magic lesson are many. Most life insurance salesmen are only "moderately" successful. They earn just a little more than the average middle-income person and if they are any happier than the average, I haven't noticed it.

Yet, every once in a while you find one insurance salesman who is going great guns and is a really top-notch earner. And in every case you'll discover the highly successful salesman puts "helping people create estates" above "earning big commissions."

Put service first, and money takes care of itself.

Do you want to find out fast why most people live the mediocre second-class life? I'll show you how you can find out. Tomorrow, pretend you're a newspaper reporter writing a feature on "Why People Get Up in the Morning." Next, stop ten people you don't know and say, "Excuse me sir, I'm writing a special report and I'd like to ask you a question. Tell me, sir, why did you get up this morning?"

The people you ask will look at you as if you're some sort of nut, but if you keep asking the question, the answers will come out.

Odds are most will tell you, "I got up this morning because I had to go to work."

Next you ask, "Why?" Here the usual answer, said in a tone that means everybody ought to know this, is, "Why, I gotta eat."

Now ask, "Why do you gotta eat?"

"So I can live," is a typical reply.

Next ask, "Why do you have to live?"

Here your friend will probably look at you with an expression that indicates his mentality has been taxed to the limit and say, "Why, so I can get up tomorrow and go to work."

This experiment will show you that most people get up in the morning because they "have to go to work" so they can "eat" so they can "live" so they can "get up and go to work the next day."

If you follow through on this experiment, you'll find most people get up to "make a living" because they "gotta eat," because "if I don't get up I'm out of a job," or because "everybody gets up in the morning."

The answers you get tell you two big facts about the way most people live. First, people are on a spiral going nowhere. They get up to go to their slave jobs so they can eat so they can keep on going to their slave jobs so they can eventually die without ever having lived.

The second fact you study of why people get up in the morning reveals is that people without a purpose go nowhere, accomplish little, and enjoy less.

Understudy the Successful: Choose a Top Notch Tutor

Let me explain an approach I've observed most successful people follow. They understudy other people who are successful.

No one can dispute this fact: We learn more from imitation than any other way. For example, chances are you speak with some type of accent or speech inflection. Most everyone does. How did you develop your speech, your tonal qualities? By *listen-*

ing and *observing* and then *imitating* someone else. Your speech, your walk, your posture, your gestures are largely adaptations from people with whom you've been closely associated.

Not only are your physical mannerisms largely a product of your past environment—your mental mannerisms are too. Your attitudes and your personal philosophy were acquired from your environment, especially the people above you—your parents, ministers, bosses.

Four years ago two young men, both students of mine, came to see me individually regarding making career connections upon finishing college. Both were intelligent, had made good grades in school, and had very similar aptitudes. Each had several job offers. At that time a very successful friend of mine with a small organization was looking for someone to serve as his assistant. I recommended each young man to my friend and urged each of them to take a look at this job.

Well, each of them took a look at the job. The first one to check it out, Jimmy Y., called me right after meeting my friend. "Dr. Schwartz," he said, in a tone of voice indicating only partially concealed disgust, "your friend is awfully tight with money. Why, he only offered me $400 a month to start. I had to turn it down flat. After all, I've already got a firm offer from another company for $600."

The next day Charles T., the other student, went out to see my friend. He too had much more lucrative offers. But he took the job. When he called me to tell me his decision, I asked him, "Does the fact that your starting pay is well below average bother you?"

His reply says a lot, "Sure, I'd like to make more money. But I'm so impressed with your friend I feel it's worth the pay difference just to learn from him. I feel he can teach me a lot and I'll be way ahead in the long run."

Well, as I said, that was 4 years ago. What's the score today? Jimmy, who started at $7,200 a year with another company is now earning $8,750. Charles, meanwhile, who started with my friend at only $4,800 is now earning $20,000 plus bonuses.

The difference? Jimmy was guided only by initial money making opportunities while Charles picked a job on the basis of what the man he would work for could teach him.

I'm often amazed at the blind approach most folks use in selecting a job. Most people try to get answers to these questions: "How much does it pay?" "What are the hours?" "What about fringe benefits?" "How many paid holidays?" and "When do I get my first automatic pay increase?"

These people—and they account for at least 90 percent—overlook the most important factor of all: *"What kind of a person will I be working for?"*

The single most important question to answer in choosing a job is this: "What can I learn from the person or persons I'll work for? What can they teach me that I can use on that job and in other jobs?"

If you were a high school football player and wanted to play pro football after college, how would you choose a college? The most important factor would be the coach who could teach you most.

I've observed that great men generally have been understudies for awhile to other great men. So, choose a man who can teach you something.

If you honestly and objectively conclude the man above you can't teach you anything, hasn't the value system you want, will not help you achieve the self-image you've projected, then move on!

Or if you wanted to become a great musician, you would select the person who most nearly fits the standard as the best. Then, you'd go to him and study.

Actors do the same thing.

No one can select his parents. But you have your choice in adult life as to who will be your *psychological* parents.

Most people give no consideration whatever to finding out what they can learn from their boss as they appraise a job. The extent of their investigation is pay, hours, holidays, fringe benefits, automatic increases.

Apply This Test

Before you go to work with anyone, ask yourself this question:

What kind of person
Would I be
If I became
Just like he?

IN QUICK REVIEW

Follow this step-by-step method to consolidate your psychic power.

1. *Decide now you will not be haunted by "The Saddest Words of Tongue or Pen Are These, It Might Have Been."*

2. *Psychologically, break the bonds of slavery.*

3. *Cure yourself of goal alibitis. It is foolish and futile to think*

A. *"I've been trained for one profession so I must stay in it."*

B. *"I can't make it on my own." You* can!

C. *"I'm too old to start over."*

D. *"I don't like my job but it's what my parents wanted."*

E. *"I've got a good job now. I'd be a fool to give it up." (Remember, a bird in the hand is* not *worth two in the bush.)*

4. *Draw up a will for living.*

5. *Discover the fact that money, lots of it, can be made in all occupations.*

6. *Remember the magic lesson for earning money:* Put service first and money takes care of itself.

7. *Understudy successful people. Choose a topnotch tutor.*

Other recommended books...

THE MYSTICAL POWER OF PYRAMID ASTROLOGY

HOW TO CHANNEL AWESOME COSMIC ENERGY

Norvell. Chants, personal mantras and meditations for raising your energy levels to meet life's every need! Shows how to chart a Karmic birthpath and analyse character; how to direct cosmic energy from the Pyramids into the higher mind centres to attract riches and abundance; and how to achieve the great destiny for which you were born. Learn also the Karmic strengths and weaknesses of your husband or wife, your children, your friends. business associates, romantic partners, social companions!

HOW TO DEVELOP A SUPER POWER MEMORY

Harry Lorayne. However poor you may *think* your memory is now, the author believes that you have a memory *10 to 20 times more powerful than you realize!* He maintains that your memory is working at a tiny fraction of its true power today—because *you simply don't know the right way to feed it facts!* Because you don't know the right way to take names and faces and anything else you want to remember—*and burn them into your memory so vividly that you can never forget them!* The most practical, lucid and effective memory-training book ever published.

IN SEARCH OF THE HEALING ENERGY

Mary Coddington. *Your* illnesses could be cured by acupuncture, homoeopathy, Reichian therapeutics, and other therapies described here—all employing healing energy emanating from one's own body! This force penetrates everything. Hahnemann termed it *the vital force*, Reich, *orgone energy*. These rays prove that the human body is as much energy (waves) as it is mass (solid particles). Now discover what this power can do for *you*! *Amazing contents include:* How acupuncture cures by balancing the body's *ch'i* energy; Homoeopathic drugs stimulate self-cure; Did Wilhelm Reich find the secret of creation?

TELECULT POWER

The Amazing New Way to Psychic and Occult Wonders

Reese P. Dubin. Reveals how to bring about any event or condition you wish—quickly, easily—by unobserved means! This is the *occult* way of achieving fame, fortune and happiness! *Magical contents include:* HOW TO—make yourself invisible; Make a magic 'money bag' in which to receive gifts from the invisible world; Read thoughts; Move objects without touching them; Make the crystal ball work for you; Use your mental levitating finger in games of chance; Tune the picture on your psychic tele-viewer!

THE BOOK OF THE SACRED MAGIC OF ABRA-MELIN THE MAGE

S. L. MacGregor-Mathers. Samuel MacGregor-Mathers (1854-1918) was a founder and chief of the Hermetic Order of the Golden Dawn. While researching rare books in magic at the Bibliotheque de l'Arsenal in Paris he was told about an eighteenth-century French manuscript, supposedly the translation of a Hebrew magical textbook written in 1458. Mathers translated the manuscript into English and this book is the result. Abra-Melin contains magical squares or talismans. Each square represents a mental or physical asset, a disease or illness to be cured, the ability to overcome natural laws, and so on. *Contents include:* How to fly in the Air; How to open every kind of lock without a Key.

GETTING WHAT YOU WANT

YOUR KEY TO LIFE AT THE TOP

J. H. Brennan. Reveals a revolutionary *four-word secret* which — translated into dynamic power-play techniques — can transform today's daydreams into the glittering reality of tomorrow — riches, prestige, popularity — even fame! *Includes:* A problem-solving technique so simple you won't believe it!; A job-application letter so powerful you'll be virtually assured of the job before the interview!; How power-play domination can guarantee you the job *at* the interview; The principles of power-play; The difference between 'dominant' and 'domineering'; Climbing the corporate ladder; Most of your colleagues harbour a 'guilty secret'; Your first Board meeting.

INSTANT MIND POWER

PROGRAMME YOUR MIND FOR SUCCESS!

Harry Lorayne. Not a book in the normal sense of the word, but a series of over 2,300 simple interlocking exercises to help you—

- **BUILD A WILL OF IRON**
- **CREATE WINNING IDEAS**
- **DEVELOP CONCENTRATION**
- **BREAK BAD HABITS**
- **FLASH-LEARN ANYTHING**
- **DEVELOP OBSERVATION**

You, the reader, actively participate in this unique programme by providing written answers to key questions. Gradually, as the power of your mind builds and expands like a giant dynamo gaining momentum, you can create a powerful success pattern—and even make one hour do the work of two!

THE MAGIC OF THE RUNES

THEIR ORIGINS AND OCCULT POWER

Michael Howard. Fascinating introduction to the history, development and magical use of the runic alphabet, an ancient form of writing shrouded in mystery. Includes detailed instructions for casting the runes for purposes of divination. The runes were used by initiates of occult traditions to pass on magical information. The unusual angular strokes of the runes is probably due to the fact that they were originally hewn into stone, thus precluding curves and rounded letters. *Other contents:* Secret of the shamans; Odin the man; Regalia of the rune masters; Origins of Ogham script; Druidic tree alphabet.

PRACTICAL TECHNIQUES OF ASTRAL PROJECTION

Dr Douglas Baker. *Illustrated.* In astral projection consciousness vacates the physical body and temporarily inhabits an astral (emotional) body which possesses its own organs of sensation! Author—who has experienced "many thousands of astral projections"—describes five stages of this phenomenon and explains the necessary routines for projecting to each stage in turn through relaxation, visualization and breathing techniques. In addition to providing historic examples of astral projection (including astral manifestations in the House of Commons), Dr Baker relates some of his own experiences while travelling on the astral plane.

THE OPENING OF THE THIRD EYE

Dr Douglas Baker. *Illustrated.* The human brain is a million pound computer which lies perfectly maintained but almost silent. This dynamic book provides five safe techniques for arousing the Third Eye (an 'inner vision' organ)for the purpose of developing a vortex of psychic energy and extending awareness into new and exciting dimensions! Highly praised by many great yogis for his occult teachings, Dr Baker has practised these techniques 'without hazard and with many rewards for over twenty years.' Includes information on the seven 'chakras' or force centres from which the Third Eye derives its power.

YOUR PSYCHIC POWERS

And How to Develop Them
Hereward Carrington Ph.D. The *only* detailed instruction manual of its kind for developing trance-mediumship! This amazing book, written by a dedicated psychical researcher, was based on notes he wrote for circulation amongst members of New York psychical societies. Introduces the whole range of psychic manifestations, including the human aura, telepathy, clairvoyance, crystal gazing, automatic writing, obsession and insanity, hypnotism and mesmerism, astral projection, spirit- and thought-photography and materialization. Guidance is also given in distinguishing between true and false phenomena. Dr. Carrington maintained: **'. . . we are all more or less mediumistic or psychic, and need only to cultivate our powers in order to develop them, and bring them to maturity.'**

AMAZING SECRETS OF THE MYSTIC EAST

Norvell. World-renowned astrologer and psychic reveals mystical secrets for transforming you life. The powerful rituals show you how to:
- **Attract Abundant Wealth**
- **Find Your Soul Mate**
- **Overcome Bad Habits**
- **Keep Young and Healthy**
- **Achieve Astral Projection**
- **Predict Your Future**

In just a few minutes a day—says Norvell—you will be able to tap the highest powers of the universe that can motivate your life in any direction you choose.

MIRACLE POWER
OF THE I CHING
ACHIEVE YOUR DREAMS—EFFORTLESSLY!

Norvell. With this book, two coins, and a single dice, you can make the I Ching—ancient Chinese Book of Changes—solve your problems and materialize your most urgent needs! The I Ching will tell you how to build a fortune, find your true soul mate, have perfect health, overcome smoking, drinking, or drug dependence, how to destroy Black Magic forces which may be working against you. The method is easy, automatic, with no complicated rituals!

MASKS OF THE SOUL
THE FACTS BEHIND REINCARNATION

Benjamin Walker. Provides essential facts relevant to reincarnation, with 'for' and 'against' evidence, including such classic case histories as Shanti Devi, Edgar Cayce, Bridey Murphy, Arthur Guirdham, and Joan Grant. With a bibliography of over 200 items, this book is the ideal introduction to a concept that is receiving increasing publicity and gaining world-wide converts. *Other contents:* Reasons for re-embodiment; The post-death experience; Hinduism and Buddhism; Transmigration of souls; The Islamic view; Christianity and reincarnation; Spiritualism and Theosophy; The Bloxham tapes; The power of suggestion; Paramnesia and Cryptomnesia; The Collective Unconscious; Karma; Other worlds.

HOW TO DEVELOP
CLAIRVOYANCE

W. E. Butler. A veteran occultist explains clairvoyance. He also provides training techniques for developing the clairvoyant powers we all possess, but which have become dormant after centuries of neglect. The book includes detailed instructions for scrying (crystal-gazing), and author reveals how to construct four satisfactory substitutes for a crystal, as crystals are expensive to purchase—but not essential in order to experience the fascinating psychic 'vision' described in these pages.

THE HEALING SECRET
OF THE AGES

Catherine Ponder. This secret is that you have 12 dynamic mind powers which are located—not in the brain—but in 12 dominant nerve centres throughout the body. Author shows how to release them for vital healing! *Contents include:* How to develop and release faith; The mysterious judgement centre within you; How to call on God's will for you; The highest form of effective prayer; Soul intensity and your five senses; Master plan for lifelong good health.

BRING OUT THE MAGIC IN YOUR MIND

Al Koran. Money! Stacks of it! Wads of crisp notes and bags of shining silver. At the right time you will get it, if you believe. This book explains unseen powers that already exist in your own mind and which can be harnessed to bring you prosperity, success, health, vitality and good looks! Koran, known as The World's Greatest Mind Reader, shows how to **bring out** this magic from your mind and **make it work for you**. He also demonstrates how to utilize astrology, numerology, colours and talismans for greater happiness and wealth. *Incredible contents include:* The secret of wealth; The magic of visualization; How belief works; The magic of love; Power of the subconscious; The magic of music; Health that brings magic; The magic of laughter; Help through your hobby; The magic of colour; Observing the wonderful; Preludes to mind-reading—physiognomy, numerology, astrology.

EXPERIMENTAL MAGIC
RELAXATION, MEDITATION, INNER PLANE CONTACT!

J. H. Brennan. Part One explains some of the phenomena found in Low (or lesser) Magic. These include the chakras, the aura, the Qabalah, astral and etheric bodies, wood nymphs and leprechauns, mantra chanting, water and ghost divining. Part Two introduces the more high-powered system of High Magic. The correct mental preparation before undertaking ritual magic is disclosed, together with information on establishing Inner Plane contact. Detailed rituals are given for assuming a godform and achieving the almost unbelievable—a state of invisibility. (A reversal ritual for regaining visibility is also provided by the author).

PYRAMID POWER
SECRET ENERGY OF THE ANCIENTS REVEALED

M. Toth & G. Nielsen. The most up-to-date source material available on pyramidology! Gives detailed instructions for 3 methods of pyramid construction. Pyramids—even cardboard ones—generate physical and ,spiritual energy, preserve foodstuffs, sharpen razor blades, stimulate psychic power! Also reveals the results of some fascinating experiments and suggests a number of simple experiments for the reader—which scientists have performed in their laboratories.

PENDULUM POWER
YOUR ENTRANCE INTO THE WORLD OF INTUITIVE AWARENESS

G. Nielsen & J. Polansky. How to make a pendulum and practise mysterious radiesthesia! Choose a career, find romance, pin-point physical and mental illness, enhance *all* aspects of living—with pendulum power! Here is a practical overview for beginners in this master science in which Higher Intelligence communicates through the nervous system, using a pendulum to amplify the signal—a new way of using the mind. *Contents include:* Why the pendulum works; True stories of pendulum power; The pendulum, your work and your career; The pendulum and dynamic self-healing; The pendulum and meditation.